DAVID PEPIN

Discovering
Shrines and Holy Places

THE RESOURCE ROOM
CHURCH HOUSE
9 THE CLOSE
WINCHESTER
SO23 9LS

SHIRE PUBLICATIONS LTD

Contents

For June, Nicholas and Thomas

ACKNOWLEDGMENTS
The cover illustration is an old print of Christchurch Priory, Dorset. Photographs are acknowledged as follows: Cadbury Lamb, plates 4, 5, 6, 7, 8, 10, 11, 12, 14, 15, 16, 18, 19, 20, 21, 22, 24; June and David Pepin, plates 1, 2, 3, 13, 17, 23, 25; David Uttley, plate 9.

Set in 9 on 9 point English roman and printed in Great Britain by C. I. Thomas & Sons (Haverfordwest) Ltd, Press Buildings, Merlins Bridge, Haverfordwest.

Introduction

In this short guide to shrines and holy places in Britain and
Northern Ireland I have chosen to journey through time, turning
the pages of history and pinpointing the main events and places
and the key figures in Britain's Christian story.

As someone who has lived in a holy place, near a celebrated
shrine, within a stone's throw of where Britain's first Christian
martyr crossed the river to his death, I have chosen to start where I
am. For the purpose of this book this is indeed a happy coin-
cidence. The writing of the book itself has been something of a
pilgrimage with plenty of good companions en route. I am grateful
to the many fellow travellers who have written about churches. I
would also like to thank the many friends, acquaintances and
custodians of cathedral and parish churches who, as always, have
shared so willingly their experiences and knowledge of our
Christian heritage. Their names are too numerous to record here,
except that I acknowledge a debt of gratitude to my wife, June,
and my typist, Lilian Griffin.

In case the word *shrine* puts some people off I should say I have
used the term in its widest sense, although I do include places
traditionally associated with saints and visionary experiences. As
for *holy places* their consideration here has had a similarly broad
treatment covering all the main Christian denominations; holy
places common to all, such as those connected with the Holy Bible,
are also referred to. Many places not mentioned in the text are
included in the gazetteer and maps.

One of the main hazards to battle with on the journey has been
the need to be selective. A glance at the maps, however, will show
that there are many and varied things to see. The British Isles are
especially rich in Christian history; one can hardly turn the corner
of a country lane, climb a hill or reach a river settlement large or
small without encountering some reminder of our roots. One has
only to contemplate visiting all the cathedral churches and chapels
and the thousands of parish churches throughout these islands to
realise what an impossible task that would be. And yet that is
where our roots lie and we do well to realise their true worth now.
In his book *Footholds in the Faith* Peter Moore, Dean of St
Albans, reminds us of our need for roots. 'What we have to do is to
use the inheritance, explore it as part of our adventure forward,'
he says.

I trust the reader will find the following essentially subjective
record of a pilgrimage to shrines and holy places an en-
couragement to discover and enjoy the same for himself or herself
and also find much more besides. May your 'adventure forward'
be one of fulfilment in every way.

1. The early centuries

And did those feet in ancient time

On a summer's day about AD 209 a man walked to his death on a hill some twenty or so miles north-west of London. This hill is today a very holy place, the site of one of the most impressive Christian shrines in Europe, a site which can justifiably claim to be the oldest continuously used site for Christian worship in Britain. The man was Alban, a citizen of the neighbouring Roman town of Verulamium, and he is known as Britain's first Christian martyr. A vast cathedral and abbey church stands on the gentle slopes of this Hertfordshire hill today, the centre of a varied ministry to the city, diocese and indeed the world at large. **St Albans** has become the focus of pilgrims and tourists from all over the world and although it could be argued that Alban is a local saint and martyr, yet the dedication appears, surprisingly, as far away as New Zealand and Australia.

Christianity probably came to Britain in the second century AD and there is evidence that it spread quickly. Unknown soldiers, slaves and traders were among those early believers. By the beginning of the fourth century Christian churches and chapels were fairly widespread; there were bishops, pastors, teachers and priests. From time to time persecution reared its ugly head and it was during one such purge that a fugitive priest was sheltered by Alban, who became a convert and within a short while exchanged places with him and was arrested in the disguise of the priest. Such persecutions and martyrdoms served to strengthen the Church. The Christian writer, Tertullian of Carthage, North Africa, was one of the first to comment that there were Christians in Britain at the extremity of the Roman Empire, and he acknowledged that 'the blood of the martyrs is seed'.

Another link which the Church in Britain has with the early Christian communities of the Middle East is in the person of Irenaeus. He became Bishop of Lyons and as a missionary in Gaul, present-day France, he became familiar with the Celtic language and its world, an important strand in Britain's Christian history, especially in the western and northern regions. Irenaeus was a pupil of the great martyr saint Polycarp, who in turn had been a disciple at the feet of St John, one of our Lord's closest apostles.

Mention must be made of St Joseph of Arimathea, who also takes us back to the first century within a generation of the Resurrection of Christ. Although Joseph is acknowledged to be an historical figure, many scholars claim that the story of his association with **Glastonbury** in Somerset should not be accepted as factual, beautiful though the legend may be. It is said that Joseph was driven off course round Land's End into the Bristol

Channel. He was accompanied on his long journey by twelve companions. They came ashore on the then island of Glastonbury, the Isle of Avalon or Isle of Apples; Joseph's staff, planted in the ground, later blossomed forth into the now famous Holy Thorn. The Holy Grail or Chalice, used at the Last Supper, was brought by him, it is said, and buried here too. It has been suggested that it is more likely that the faith came to Glastonbury on the lips of persecuted Christians who crossed the Channel from France and in particular from the areas of persecution in south-eastern Gaul. Be that as it may, Glastonbury has a memorable Christian tradition and deserves a place on the itinerary of all earnest pilgrims. More will be said about this holy place later. There are also references to Joseph's visits, apparently as a trader, accompanied by Jesus as a boy, and one or two places in the West Country recall these.

An event of profound significance took place in October 312. It has come down to us partly as legend, although the influence it had was by no means legendary or unimportant. Constantine had been Emperor for six years, having been declared so in York, where his father had died whilst they were both on a visit to Britain. At that time they were pagans and were responsible for the deaths of many Christians. Back in Italy, in an effort to establish his rule amidst rival claimants, he was about to march on Rome when, according to the now famous story, he was confronted with a great flaming cross in the noonday sky. 'By this sign conquer' was the challenge and later that night in a dream he was urged to emblazon his banner with the Christian monogram Chi Rho, the first two letters of the Greek word for Christ. Whatever the truth of the matter, Constantine certainly experienced a profound spiritual awakening; he obeyed the vision, won the battle against his rival and steadfastly set his mind to supporting the Christian cause, now that he was supreme ruler in the west. After Christianity had received state approval, the Church was to experience certain setbacks and evils which it has never really overcome. The Faith was to enjoy complete freedom throughout the Empire and Sunday became the official 'day of rest' and prayer.

There are still a few reminders of the early Christians in Roman Britain. At **Lullingstone** in the beautiful Darent valley, in north-west Kent, are the excavated remains of a Roman villa, said to have been the property of a Christian family in the fourth century, possibly about 380. It possesses a little private chapel especially adapted and probably one of the earliest. There is some wall plaster depicting Christians at prayer with arms raised, and also the Christian Chi Rho sign. This is attractive downland country through which passes the ancient North Downs Way, to be frequented later by pilgrims.

> And did those feet in ancient time
> Walk upon England's mountains green;
> And was the Holy Lamb of God
> On England's pleasant pastures seen.

Such words come easily to mind here in this splendid walking country. Their author, William Blake, mystical poet and painter, stayed once at neighbouring **Shoreham** with the visionary painter Samuel Palmer. **Eynsford** village is a little closer to this ancient Christian site at Lullingstone and, fourteen centuries after the Roman Christians, the Christian message was proclaimed here by John Wesley. He is said to have stood by the picturesque ford and bridge to preach.

Silchester, in present-day north Hampshire, stood at the meeting point of two ancient tracks. It was the site of a Celtic earthwork and the Romans established a small town here, calling it Calleva Atrebatum. Sometime in the fourth century a small Christian church was built within its walls, one of the few churches (as opposed to Christian chapels) built during the Roman occupation. The town now lies beneath fields, although excavations have taken place. The medieval church of St Mary stands today almost on the old wall.

From time to time the pilgrim will come across Christian features dating from Roman times but they are rare. At **Hinton St Mary** in Dorset, for example, there was found a fourth-century mosaic of Christ between two pomegranates.

In all probability St Martin's Church at **Canterbury** in Kent was founded soon after the death of the great missionary himself. After his experience with the beggar and his conversion, Martin eventually became Bishop of Tours in France, and this he remained until his death in 397 at the age of sixty-two. He is regarded as the pioneer of monasticism in the west. Known as the patron saint of France, Martin became famous all over northern Europe and many churches in Britain were named after him. The one in ancient, beautiful Canterbury and the one 'in the Fields' by Trafalgar Square in **London** are among the best known. It is fitting that the latter has always had a special ministry to the 'down and outs' and underprivileged, recalling the saint's experience of old. St Martin's-in-the-Bull Ring, **Birmingham,** also plays a prominent role in Christian witness.

In the year that Martin died a monk called Ninian crossed the desolate region near Hadrian's Wall and settled in the lowlands of present-day Scotland. The wall is probably the most spectacular relic of Roman Britain; it was the north-west boundary of the Empire. This was indeed the back of beyond and even today the modern traveller may well feel something of the pioneer spirit and apprehension which the evangelising Ninian would have experienced, in a countryside of solitude and ruggedness, and under threat of attack from the wild Picts — the *picti* or woad-painted men — he came to convert. Ninian, the son of a chief, was born about 360. He visited Rome and also met Martin of Tours, learning about missionary strategy, using monks to evangelise locally from a Christian outpost. Ninian, therefore, brought Martin's system to Galloway, where he built a church of white stone, Candida Casa — the White House, which he used as a base. Ruins of the church of **Whithorn** Priory still possibly contain his tomb. Pilgrims travelling by sea would come ashore at a safe harbour at the Isle of Whithorn to the south-east, where there are ruins of a medieval kirk of St Ninian. St Ninian's Cave overlooks a peaceful stretch of beach about four miles west, and here pilgrims today pay their respects in this holy place where the saint himself prayed.

The Greek word *monos* means alone, and the first monks, or solitaries, lived in caves in Egypt. St Anthony is regarded as the very first hermit to do this, in the mid third century. As has been mentioned, St Martin is generally thought of as the man who introduced this eastern desert way of life to the west and he is known to have settled in caves himself on the banks of the river Loire and elsewhere, as did his followers. As in the east, the communal or monastic life developed and spread all over Europe and the splendid heritage left to us of this enterprise is with us still in the great monastic churches. However, a simple cave can still evoke that same sense of awe and wonder for the infinite that the early monks, such as Ninian, sought. Nothing is too mundane or ordinary to be a holy place, as we shall often discover.

Ninian worked for well over thirty years among the Picts in eastern Scotland. His influence also spread to the Scots of the west and in Ireland; the Scots were originally inhabitants of Ireland. Places as far north as **Shetland** also recall Ninian, the Apostle of Scotland. He died in 432, the year in which, by tradition, Patrick returned to Ireland as Bishop.

Patrick, Ireland's patron saint, was a Briton, born about 385, somewhere in the west, 'between Clyde and Severn estuary' (Glamorgan perhaps). He was captured as a youth by Scots slave traders from the north of Ireland, he escaped to the continent, was trained as a priest in one of St Martin's schools in Gaul, returned home and was urged in a dream to return to Ireland. Sir Arthur Bryant in his *Story of England* reminds us that this story is 'one of the great stories of mankind'. Indeed, its impact was later to be felt all over these islands. In the north of Ireland he preached throughout Ulster and traditionally is said to have been instrumental in banishing all snakes and venomous reptiles. The cathedral city of **Downpatrick** is of very ancient origin, pleasantly situated at the south-western tip of Strangford Lough, a few miles

7

in from the coast. The present Church of Ireland cathedral stands on the site of an abbey said to have been founded by St Patrick. It is, however, by no means certain that the rugged granite boulder in the graveyard inscribed *Patrick* marks the site of the saint's relics and also those of two other Irish patrons, St Bridget and St Columba. The abbey ruins a mile or so north-east of the city at **Sabhal** (a barn) or Saul mark another holy place because it was where Patrick supposedly held his first Christian service on Irish soil in 432 and also where he died twenty-nine years later. Just beyond **Slieve Patrick** nearby stands a memorial shrine and at **Struel** (meaning stream) just east of Downpatrick are holy wells associated with the saint. **Raholp,** about two miles from Saul, boasts one of Ireland's oldest buildings, Church-moyley, very small and probably founded by St Patrick. Here we are not far from the place where he stepped ashore.

Pilgrims are well advised to acquaint themselves with the district since there is much of interest connected both directly and indirectly with this great figure in Christian history, although the main pilgrimage centre is at **Croagh Patrick**, an impressive mountain across the border in County Mayo to the west. Here the saint observed Lent in 441. Over seventy-five thousand pilgrims, many barefooted, visit this holy place on the last Sunday in July every year, Garland Sunday. Just across the border in Donegal in the Red Lake — **Lough Derg** — is an island where in a cave, Caverna Purgatorii, Patrick had a vision of purgatory, it is claimed. Pilgrims still go in penitence today.

The city of **Armagh** is the ecclesiastical capital of Ireland. Here is the seat of both the Archbishops, of the Church of Ireland and of the Roman Catholic Church. Armagh's history goes back before Christ and, as far as the Christian faith is concerned, it is older than Canterbury. Patrick, it is believed, chose this site for the start of his mission and here he founded a church in 432. This Church of Ireland cathedral, medieval and restored, is at the very centre of the city. The Roman Catholic cathedral, begun on St Patrick's Day 1840, graces Knockadrain Hill to the north-west. Ancient and modern combine to remind us that this countryside rich in Christian history (to quote Sir Arthur Bryant again) 'instead of slavers . . . exported saints and missionaries to convert others'. While Patrick and his followers 'preached peace to you who were far off and peace to those who were near' (Ephesians 2), the Saxon invaders were wiping out every vestige of learning and civilisation in southern and eastern Britain.

2. 500 to 700

The flags of dawn appear

We shall now see where and how the light of faith, albeit dim in places, was kept burning.

One stormy night early in the sixth century, somewhere on the rugged coast of Menavia in south-west Wales, the Christian daughter of a chieftain gave birth to a son. She was Nonna and her son was called Dewi or David. The storm raged; so did King Sant of that region of Wales. On hearing of the imminent birth of a child of great power he determined to slay it. However, the storm forced everyone to remain indoors. The holy place where David was born was 'bathed in brilliant light'. Today, one can walk about a mile to the south of **St David's** cathedral and enjoy part of the coastal path, with exhilarating views of the cliffs and sea, feeling something of the eternal ruggedness and simple beauty which inspired the Celtic church. One can also visit **St Non's Well**, carefully preserved nearby, and a little further on the chapel which marks the traditional site of the birth of the patron saint of Wales. In addition to the splendid St David's cathedral church in the lonely valley called Glyn Rhosyn, a memorable shrine which possesses the saint's bones, there are well over fifty churches in South Wales named after him. There are also several churches dedicated to him both in Cornwall and Brittany. Dewi Sant, as he is known in Wales, travelled far: to Crowland in Lincolnshire, to Glastonbury in Somerset, where he founded a little church, and to neighbouring Bath also. David died at a ripe old age in 601, in his own monastery.

At the time of David's birth there were already Christians in Wales. As Roman influence declined, Christianity had gained ground. Gildas, the historian, was born on Clydeside and studied in South Wales. He writes as a witness about the warlike barbarians overrunning Britain at a time when cries for help fell on deaf ears. Rome itself was also fighting for survival. The legions had been called home. Christians were being slaughtered 'as lambs by butchers'. However, although this period is often called the Dark Ages in England, in the Celtic west, in Wales, Cornwall and Ireland, it is the Age of Saints, a time of growth for the Church. In North Wales, **Bangor** Cathedral can justly lay claim to be the oldest cathedral foundation in Britain. A monastery was founded here in 525. St Deiniol was bishop in 545. The fabric of the cathedral church today is of more recent date.

In the west, with its estuaries and river systems, travel and communications were good. There was frequent coming and going between Ireland, western Britain and Brittany on the European mainland. In 550 a boatload of fifty scholars and monks landed in southern Ireland. We have already seen what effective work was done by earnest evangelists such as Ninian and Patrick. There were scores of lesser mortals, local men and women of God about whom countless legends are told to colour the tapestry of our early history. These saints have been likened to worker priests of the present century, participating in the day-to-day life of the people they served, and retreating from time to time into isolation. Hermits sought sanctuary and time to commune with the infinite in remote valleys and isolated storm-beaten islands bordering the Atlantic. There is a strange paradox in this: involvement and yet isolation — seemingly lonely souls, wandering in search of the abundant life. We come across their holy wells, innumerable holy places on rocky headlands and in sheltered coombs, their simple oratories and beehive cells reminding all of the rigorous unencumbered lifestyle of Christian discipleship, and their wheel-head crosses of austere granite still in part fulfilling their purpose. Villages have often grown up around these holy places and their names are often most unusual to the foreigner-pilgrim today. Celtic missionary monks would approach a local chief to build a church surrounded by their little huts or cells. In Wales the settlement was called a *llan*, which is still the Welsh word for church or parish. Teilo, a sixth-century monk, worked near the river Taff and his *llan* was sited where **Llandaff** Cathedral, splendidly restored after bomb damage, stands today, just north-west of Cardiff.

It was around this period that the events which gave rise to the Arthurian legend took place. There is plenty of substantial evidence to guide us through the mythical trappings which enveloped the person of Arthur, the Past and Future King. At **Tintagel** on the north Cornish coast is his reputed birthplace. The rocky peninsula is the site of a sixth-century fortress. Celtic monks also had cells on the precipitous rock. While in this region the pilgrim would do well to visit **St Pirian-in-the-Sand**, Perran-zabuloe, a little to the south-west of Newquay. The so-called 'lost church' of St Pyran (Pirian) is today protected from further submergence beneath the windswept sands, but the atmosphere amidst the dunes with larks and gulls overhead is such that one can feel something of those far off Celtic endeavours when Arthur, and Pyran too, were battling against all odds, fortified by the Christian ideal. Other places in the West Country such as **Glastonbury**, on the Isle of Avalon, have associations with Arturius, this 'king' who won a decisive victory at Mount Badon, as a result of which the Faith was able to survive, for a few decades at least. Disaster and decay, however, loomed constantly on the eastern horizon and finally won the day. The Angles and Saxons settled. The true Britons were comparatively safe and well provided for spiritually in the remote mountainous regions of the West. Here the Faith survived. Eastern and southern England, or 'Angleland', needed a new crusade.

The faith which never tires

St Martin's Church in **Canterbury,** Kent, is said to be the oldest church in constant use in England, dating from before the mission of St Augustine from Rome in 597. It is a simple building with a dark, evocative interior. Here the Christian Queen Bertha, formerly of the Frankish royal house and wife of the pagan King Ethelbert, worshipped even before her husband was converted. This church, according to the Venerable Bede writing his famous *History of the English Church and People* in the early eighth century, was 'built in honour of St Martin' during the Roman occupation of Britain, as we have already seen.

'Angels not Angles' is the famous comment which has come down to us from the Roman market place where Abbot Gregory had caught sight of some unfortunate slaves up for sale. His 'angels' were from England and he determined there and then to reach that distant region with the good news of the gospel. It turned out that he was unable to go himself but as bishop later on he commissioned the prior of a monastery in Rome, a certain Augustine. A company of forty monks were to assist him on this vital enterprise. After a false start prompted by a mood of hesitation and fear of the unknown, they eventually crossed the Channel and landed in the kingdom of Kent at a place called **Ebbsfleet** today. Landfall and departure are much in mind here near Pegwell Bay and the Isle of Thanet, since modern hovercraft leave from close by. Half a mile inland along a lane a tall stone cross marks the place where Augustine and his monks came ashore. At times the unforgettable fragrance from the lavender field close by enhances one's pilgrimage to this holy place. Augustine was allowed to meet King Ethelbert in the open air. The company continued on its way to **Canterbury** ten miles or so further inland.

There is good reason to approach this great shrine today from the east, as Augustine did, but this is the exception rather than the rule because twentieth-century pilgrims travel usually from London or Dover. Canterbury has been called the City of Pilgrims and it is a must on every pilgrim's itinerary. Augustine's mission proved successful in Kent at least. He was the first Archbishop of Canterbury. King Ethelbert was baptised into the Faith together with many of his people and he gave land for the cathedral church. Monasteries were founded and Augustine also established bishoprics at **Rochester** and **London.** To crown his limited achievement Augustine endeavoured to establish a good relationship with other Christians in Britain, namely those of the church in Wales and the south-west. It was not to be: Augustine is supposed to have met the Celtic delegation beneath an oak tree but he failed to rise in order to greet them. This was regarded as a disrespectful attitude and set discussions on an uneasy footing at the outset. The Celtic Church was not prepared at this stage to submit to the Roman branch of the Faith. The place of the meeting was possibly near Cricklade on the upper reaches of the Thames or where the Anglican cathedral stands in Bristol. Other places also claim St Augustine's oak. The so called Apostle of England died in 604. He had been prior of a monastery in Rome dedicated to St Andrew, one of Christ's first apostles. It is believed that some relics of Andrew found their way to **Hexham** in Northumbria, since the abbey there was later dedicated to the saint. Subsequently the relics were borne by a king of the Picts to Scotland, where he founded the town called **St Andrews** to this day. It is to Scotland that we must now turn again but it is good to think that Augustine, who brought the Faith back to southern England, making Canterbury an ecclesiastical capital, has a link, albeit slight and indirect, with the ecclesiastical capital of Scotland. It is, however, to an island off the west coast of Scotland that we travel first.

The name of **Iona** has resounded down the centuries. Iona, the most peaceful spot in all Scotland, ranks with Jerusalem, Rome and Canterbury as a most potent force in the Christian story. Just over thirty years before Augustine stepped ashore near the Isle of Thanet in Kent, a monk known as 'the dove' stepped from his coracle on to the shore of a little island off the coast of Dalriada, the western part of present-day Scotland. Born in the north of Ireland around 521, about sixty years after Patrick's death, Columba, or Colmcille, was of noble birth. As a young priest in 546 he founded a monastery at Derry, the oak grove, upon a hill which became an easy prey for marauding Viking pirates. A thousand years later the city was renamed **Londonderry**. Wishing to be a 'pilgrim for Christ' and, some say, as an act of penance for a certain guilt he felt for the death of some fellow countrymen in a skirmish, Columba sailed with twelve monks to the little island less than a mile off the south-west of Mull: a monastery was built from which the monks set out to preach to the Picts on the mainland. In Inverness King Buda became a Christian and the mission's ripples of success reached to Orkney and Shetland, the Faroes and Hebrides; to all these outlying places came small groups of monks in their coracles. Columba died on Iona in 597, the same year that Augustine's mission began six hundred miles away in the south. Iona today is still a great Christian centre. It was for hundreds of years the island of the west 'nearest heaven', and countless souls earnestly sought the right to be buried here. For four hundred years it was the centre of Celtic Christianity. In 1938 the Iona Community was founded under the able leadership of the Reverend George MacLeod.

In 635 Aidan, another Irishman by birth, was a monk of Iona; he was summoned by King Oswald of Northumbria to inaugurate a mission and it is a mark of providence that another island retreat was available just off the north-east coast of England, a short distance from the King's castle at Bamburgh. The Holy Island of **Lindisfarne** (itself a Celtic word referring to the *Lindis* stream, which appears only at low tide near this *farne*, or land) was an ideal base from which to evangelise Northumbria. It was, however, a sitting target for plundering Norsemen in future years. The Venerable Bede writes of Oswald the most Christian king, and how, through his influence, other kingdoms were brought to a knowledge of the Faith. Incidentally, Oswald had become a Christian himself on Iona. His father-in-law was Cynegils, the first Christian king of Wessex, in the south. The heathen Penda of Mercia, however, invaded Oswald's kingdom and the latter was killed in a battle. This was probably somewhere near Oswestry. Oswald is regarded as a martyr king and there were to be others.

Lindisfarne, like Iona, is a place in which to linger—an island sanctuary and yet not an island, since a three-mile causeway connects to the mainland at low tide. The old Pilgrims' Way was a track across the sands with over two hundred poles to guide and two refuge boxes for pilgrims caught unawares! Still more remote are the little Farne Islands. On one of these was a monk's cell and this brings us to another much loved saint of northern Britain, St Cuthbert. He was born about 634. According to legend, Cuthbert, a shepherd in the Northumbrian foothills, had a vision of Aidan's soul being taken to heaven; subsequently he became a monk at Melrose on the river Tweed. Later he travelled extensively in the hill country attending to the spiritual needs of the scattered isolated people. He loved the solitary life and that is why, after Lindisfarne itself, he sought the added tranquillity of the Farne Islands. In 685 he was finally persuaded to be bishop. As death approached two years later he retired to his solitary island. His final resting place is in magnificent **Durham** Cathedral, where a simple slab of stone inscribed *CUTHBERTUS* marks his grave behind the High Altar. The massive cathedral is built on one of the most impressive sites in the world, towering majestically above the wooded slopes of the winding river Wear. It was to this strategic place that the monks eventually came after many years of wandering with blessed Cuthbert's body, faithfully seeking a refuge safe from marauding pirates.

The silent stars are strong

Another great national shrine of the north of England is **York** Cathedral, better known as York Minster. A minster is primarily a centre for mission. This vast edifice, Britain's largest medieval cathedral, grew from very humble beginnings. On Easter Day 627, in a little wooden church especially built for the purpose, the Saxon King Edwin was baptised 'with all the nobility and a large number of humbler folk'. They were baptised by Paulinus. Edwin's father-in-law was Ethelbert of Kent who had been converted by Augustine thirty years before. Edwin's wife, Ethelberga, was permitted to bring from Kent her chaplain, Bishop Paulinus, who became the first Archbishop of York as Augustine was of Canterbury. The building of a stone structure at York Minster went on apace. Paulinus, who was bishop for about six years, evangelised widely, coming as far south as Lincoln, but this happy state of affairs did not last. Edwin was killed in combat with hostile forces and Paulinus returned by sea to Kent, taking the widowed Ethelberga and her children to safety. For ten years or so he laboured untiringly as Bishop of **Rochester** in Kent; within the Saxon cathedral church here at Roffa, on the river Medway, Paulinus was buried and so too was St Ithamar, the first Englishman to become a bishop. At the west end of the beautiful Norman nave at Rochester the curved line of the apse of the Saxon cathedral is marked out in bronze. In her distress, Ethelberga was not to be deterred from worthwhile enterprise. She founded a double monastery for monks and nuns remote in the North Downs near the coast at Folkestone. The site today is marked by the little visited yet beautiful church in the village of **Lyminge**, where Ethelberga's bones were once enshrined and revered by pilgrims.

On that momentous Easter Day in 627 the young Princess Hilda, a grand niece of Edwin, was baptised as well. She became a nun and subsequently head of the famous monastery high on the cliff above the North Sea at **Whitby**. In 664 this was the venue for a great synod or meeting of church leaders. Both Celtic and southern Christians came together to resolve differences in approach and tradition. A case in point was the date for the celebration of Easter, since the Roman Church in the south and in Europe observed this festival at a different time from the Celtic north. One of the most persuasive speakers at this synod was the much travelled Abbot of Ripon, the thirty-year-old Wilfrid. The council decided to observe the various customs of the Roman Church and Wilfrid was the dominant personality. Both at **Ripon** Minster, where the pilgrim can still visit Wilfrid's simple, ancient Saxon crypt, mysteriously evocative and Roman, and at **Whitby** Abbey, a celebrated centre of learning, Celtic, windswept and open to the elements in its ruined state, one can feel something of those momentous days, for it was in holy places such as these that the two waves of missionary zeal met. Furthermore, for lovers of music and hymnody especially, Whitby is of special interest since it was here that Caedmon, the humble cowherd, acknowledged God's gift of song. Though illiterate, 'he sang about the beginning of all things'. In consequence he is known as England's first religious poet and hymn writer. Another son of the double monastery here (that is for nuns as well as monks) was the

14

celebrated John of Beverley. He set **Beverley** on the map, crowned as it is today with one of the most magnificent Gothic churches in the world; for many this comes as a delightful surprise in the somewhat secluded, fertile region of north Humberside. Here in 721 John, the former bishop of Hexham and York, died and was buried.

Wilfrid is sometimes called the 'Star' of the Saxon church. As a star he shone in several places, well scattered. France, the Netherlands and Rome all witnessed his dominant personality. This great prince of the Church is probably mostly remembered as the apostle of the South Saxons, whom, it is said, he taught the art of fishing from wicker coracles. The first cathedral church of Sussex, a Saxon building, lies beneath the sea, off **Selsey**, or Seals' Island. In this area of a wild life sanctuary, St Peter's Church is especially memorable in its picturesque remote setting. It was the Normans who transferred the bishop's church from Selsey to **Chichester**, of which more later.

A procession of twentieth-century pilgrims can sometimes be seen wending its way between fields to another little chapel, that of **St Peter-on-the-Wall**, by the Blackwater estuary in Essex. Although this is a long way from Northumbria it is nevertheless the result of a Celtic mission. The eldest of four brothers who were all priests, Cedd, was invited south to preach and teach in the kingdom of the East Saxons. That was in the mid seventh century and he had his cathedral church built on the site of the devastated Roman fort of Othona, on the coast by the Blackwater estuary. What remains today is an isolated, rugged, stone building, impressive in its simplicity: members of the nearby Othona Community, housed in hutments, use the chapel regularly. There are also diocesan pilgrimages from time to time to this ancient cathedral church. It is a sobering thought that this chapel, an ancient power house of Christian faith, still serving the purpose for which it was built, is little, if at all, overshadowed by the twentieth-century nuclear power station just round the coast at Bradwell. The lifespan of the latter is probably limited to another decade or so. Cedd founded churches elsewhere, including one at **Lastingham**, a village remote in the North Yorkshire moors. The crypt here housed his plague-ridden body, although it was buried after his death in 664 near the high altar of the abbey church.

Cedd's brother Chad succeeded him as abbot but he was later entrusted with the bishopric of Mercia, the midland kingdom. After his death in 672, his tomb in **Lichfield** Cathedral became the focus of devout pilgrims. In 1972, the thirteen hundredth anniversary, the Archbishop of Canterbury spoke of the 'gentleness and otherworldliness of Chad'. Today the cathedral's three graceful spires, familiarly known as the Ladies of the Vale, draw one to this sacred spot and to Stowe Pool, a short distance eastwards, where the saint had founded a little church and where he baptised local folk at a spring.

Another sacred spring and pool, many miles to the south-east in Kent, high on the cliff at **Folkestone**, is associated with another saint of these times. St Eanswythe is a good example of a local saint who has never acquired a widespread reputation but who, nevertheless, deserves due acknowledgement. She was the granddaughter of King Ethelbert of Kent and she became the abbess of the very first nunnery in England, just east of the present parish church overlooking the harbour and the English Channel. Eanswythe died in 640 and her shrine, comprising some of her bones in a casket, is within the sanctuary of the ancient church.

Mention of various churches such as those at Folkestone, a town, and Lyminge, a village (a pattern repeated in thousands of other places throughout Britain), reminds us that it was during the second half of the seventh century that England was divided up into small areas known as parishes which in turn were grouped together to form the dioceses. It is to an elderly bishop from Greece, Theodore, that we owe this almost unique arrangement, for which the people of Britain should ever be grateful. Theodore was appointed Archbishop of Canterbury in 668, four years after the great synod debate at Whitby when it was decided that the English church should become more closely integrated with the mainstream of the Christian Church in Europe. For the last twenty or so years of his life (he died aged ninety) he gradually instilled a sense of belonging to a wider church. Small local Christian communities began to feel united in one common purpose. Each parish had a priest in charge and each diocese a bishop, whom Theodore summoned to meetings from time to time. Such a synod was the Council of **Hertford** in 673, the first council of the whole English Church. Thus there was a church parliament before there was a state parliament. Canon J. S. Kendall in his *Short History of the Church of England* (published in 1911) points out: 'There can be no doubt that the people laid this lesson to heart and applied it later on to political affairs. English people were first taught to meet in Parliament by seeing their clergy meeting in Synods.'

Theodore's relationship with that other great figure, Wilfrid, was not always very friendly, however, but it was the latter who was associated with the founding of yet another well known Christian community, this time in East Anglia. **Ely** Cathedral is un-forgettable. The sight of the great church, shiplike, rising above the flat ocean of the surrounding fertile fens, is one of the grandest and most memorable in Britain. The fens were once undrained and most inhospitable to all but the hardiest fen dwellers among the reedy meres and pools, but it was to such a remote refuge that, in 673, a thirty-three year old princess came as a nun to found a double monastery and to be installed by her friend Wilfrid as the first abbess, which she remained until her death just six years later. Etheldreda was the daughter of an East Anglian king. Few people today would associate trinkets bought at a fair with this famous lady, but in the middle ages at St Audrey's Fair, in Ely, held in honour of Etheldreda (the same name really), there were little trinkets known as taudries, or tawdries, a word with an unfortunate connotation today. Ely has been an inspiring place of pilgrimage for over thirteen centuries and the unique central tower of this magnificent cathedral church, the octagon and lantern, crowns this much visited shrine as befits a house of God founded by a saintly princess.

Another great fenland church is **Peterborough** Cathedral, unfamiliar still to many, although it deserves a place on many a journey. A relic of Oswald, martyred king of Northumbria, was one of several relics collected together to attract pilgrims. This somewhat questionable practice was fairly commonplace, however, and in this particular case it could perhaps be justified on the grounds that it was a kinsman of King Oswald who had founded the minster in the first place. Do not miss this truly splendid church, with its majestic Norman nave and apse.

Yet another impressively sited church is **Malmesbury** Abbey, above the water meadows of the Wiltshire Avon and the little Inglebourne stream. Here Aldhelm, scholar and unconventional preacher, formerly a prince, was abbot at about this time. He is buried in the abbey. Pilgrims travelling from Malmesbury to Glastonbury worshipped at Aldhelm's little Saxon church of St Lawrence, in the beautiful Bath-stone town of **Bradford-on-Avon**. In 705 Aldhelm became the first bishop of **Sherborne** in Dorset, where his cousin, King Ina, founded an ecclesiastical centre near a clear stream, the Scire Burn. The splendid abbey as well as the well known public school and the almshouses of this delightful stone town should be visited.

It is obvious, even to the casual observer, that the British countryside is full of holy places associated with the numerous holy men and women of those distant Saxon days. The spiritual and physical energy and subsequent missionary achievements of the seventh-century Church were very considerable indeed throughout Britain.

3. 700 to 1066

Thy Kingdom come!

The attractive market town of **Crediton** among the red-soiled fields of Devon is not a place one would normally associate with the distant heathen tribes of Germany or the Frankish royal house of the late eighth century. However, a certain native of the area in those far off days became a missionary and a bishop and finally sacrificed his life for the gospel in those parts. Wynfrith, meaning joy and peace, was probably born about 680 near Crediton, where his father was a Saxon thane of the great kingdom of Wessex. He became a monk at neighbouring Exeter and later at Nursling near Southampton, where he became a scholar, compiling England's first Latin grammar. He is better known as Boniface — one who does good — presumably on account of his reputation in learning and especially missionary endeavour. His desire to serve in a wider sphere took him to the Netherlands, Rome and Germany, and he endured martyrdom finally in the Netherlands. Both Boniface of Crediton and the slightly older Willibrord from Ripon represent a change in the outlook of the English church. No longer was England needing just to receive missionaries; she was now in a position to send them forth. Boniface was even made Archbishop of Mainz and he worked with King Pepin, whom he had anointed at Soissons, to reform the Frankish kingdom. Pepin's son Charlemagne was crowned Emperor on Christmas Day 800, and again it was an Anglo-Saxon scholar, Alcuin of York, who was so influential in directing what is known as the Carolingian Renaissance. Alcuin had been master of the cathedral school in York and at the time of his death in 804 he was Abbot of Tours. England was no longer in a backwater beyond the mainstream of Christian activity. Unfortunately, Charlemagne died in 814 and the Holy Roman Empire was split and open to the merciless ravages of the pagan sea-wolves, the Vikings of the north.

In 793, the same year that a Saxon, King Offa of Mercia, was establishing a larger church and monastery on the site of the execution of Britain's first Christian martyr, Alban, a fleet of pirate ships raided the Holy Island of Lindisfarne in the far north. These Norsemen were to come again and again all around the coasts and beyond to plunder, rape and murder. 'From the fury of the Norsemen, good Lord, deliver us!' the people prayed. In three raids on Iona the pirates slaughtered seventy monks, a horror commemorated by Martyrs' Bay. Other parts of Scotland and Ireland were not immune from this terror of the longships.

Much of great beauty was lost to flame and plunder but two famous manuscripts have survived, namely the Book of Kells and the Lindisfarne Gospel. The name most often associated with manuscripts of the period is Bede, the historian. Far away in Europe his reputation had earned him the name Venerable, by which he is generally known. All books had to be written out by hand, and consequently hundreds of monks skilled in writing and illumination worked at this painstaking task, and the results still to be seen today in certain cathedral libraries and museums are very beautiful and priceless. Bede died a little more than fifty years before the Viking invasions started in earnest. He passed his entire adult life in the monastery at **Jarrow**, a twin house to that at **Monkwearmouth**, where he had been taken as a little orphan. His contemporary Boniface called him 'a light of the church, lit by the Holy Spirit'. When one considers that he travelled hardly at all, his translation of the Bible, historical and prose writings, letters and homilies are all the more remarkable. His influence reached far and wide; he was the head of the monastery school, which had, even in those days, as many as six hundred boys. He is known as the Father of English History and in his great work *The History of the English Church and People* he gathers together stories from all over the country. He died at Jarrow in 735, and his tomb, together with that of Cuthbert, that other great northern saint, can be seen in **Durham** Cathedral.

Saxon monasteries continued to educate scholars and, in addition to the Northumbrian schools, there were several other good ones such as those at **Dunwich** in East Anglia, **Malmesbury** in Wiltshire and **Canterbury**. The Viking onslaught soon put paid to much of this in the ninth century but there arose a figure in the nick of time, the only English king to be honoured with the tital Great. He was Alfred of Wessex, who ruled during the last quarter of the ninth century.

Alfred visited the Pope in Rome at the age of five, no doubt in the company of the court tutor, Bishop Swithun. This popular saint of Wessex, traditionally referred to as the Rain Saint from his legendary connection with a period of forty wet days after his feast day, 15th July, travelled widely throughout his diocese, preaching and caring for his flock in those dangerous times. He was himself a lad of about nine, attending the monastery school in the Wessex capital of **Winchester** at the time of Charlemagne's death on the Continent. Swithun's shrine in Europe's longest medieval cathedral at Winchester is of a very distinctive modern design. In the middle ages this ancient city was on many a pilgrim route and it still is today. Whilst at Winchester a pleasant stroll by the river brings the pilgrim to St Cross Hospital, where pensioners still live in the ancient almshouses. The Wayfarer's Dole of bread and ale is still received by grateful pilgrims!

Alfred was born at Wantage in 849 and became king at the age of twenty-two in 871. He pursued a determined campaign to make a lasting peace with the Viking army under its leader Guthrum. In the period before his final victory at Ethandune, or **Edington** — well worth a visit for its beautiful priory church — Alfred's time of preparation in the secluded marshes of Somerset is shrouded in the mists of legend but **Athelney**, the Isle of Nobles, and its neighbourhood still possess a special atmosphere and holy places associated with this great Christian king. The little 'island' town of **Wedmore** witnessed the signing of the famous peace treaty in 878.

Guthrum agreed to accept the Christian faith and was duly baptised together with many of his men, some say at **Aller** in Somerset, or perhaps at **Chippenham.** In his hour of victory Alfred showed great magnanimity and saved England, though it was divided into the Saxon kingdoms and the Danelaw, from becoming completely pagan again.

Alfred greatly encouraged learning and craftsmanship. He welcomed scholars from far afield. Such a companion was the Welsh monk Bishop Asser, Alfred's scribe and close friend, who helped him with translations of such works as the Bible and Bede's *History.* A new project was the Anglo-Saxon Chronicle, copies of which were made and kept up to date for some considerable time in the monasteries of Peterborough, Winchester and York. Alfred, 'the Protector of the Poor', died in 901, but his grave near the ancient Hyde Abbey in **Winchester** is now unknown. His feast day however, 26th October, just after United Nations Day, is a most appropriate time to recall his greatness with gratitude, since he had, above all, a profound unifying and reconciling influence.

As has already been noted, churches, monasteries and schools all needed refounding or establishing from scratch. **Shaftesbury** Abbey, in the Dorset hilltop town where memorable Gold Hill overlooks the Blackmoor Vale, is now but a ruin, a pleasant gardenlike site, but it was probably Alfred's grandest foundation; dating from 880, this nunnery's first abbess was Alfred's daughter. Just over 150 years later, King Canute died here but was finally laid to rest in Winchester, along with Saxon kings and bishops. St Edward, king and martyr, was buried at Shaftesbury after his body was removed from **Wareham.** At the age of eighteen in 978 this young king was cruelly murdered at **Corfe,** as a result of a royal family feud. His tomb was much revered at Shaftesbury; he was regarded as a young martyr not so much for his Christian faith but because he was killed so unjustly. His stepmother, Queen Elfreda, founded a monastery two years later, at **Amesbury.** The dedication to St Melor of Brittany is appropriate. He was a young man who died in similar circumstances. It was to the great monastery here in earlier times, famous for its three hundred strong Choir of Ambrosius, that Arthur's queen, Guinevere, came as abbess.

Other kings suffered ignoble deaths and in consequence were honoured as martyrs. Two of the most famous are St Ethelbert and St Edmund. Towards the close of the eighth century, Ethelbert, a young Christian king of East Anglia, was put to death by trickery, perpetrated by Offa of Mercia, whose daughter was about to marry Ethelbert. The evil deed was carried out at Sutton Walls, near **Hereford,** and the body was buried secretly by the river Ludd. Offa later regretted the deed and promptly, for peace of mind, and no doubt to ensure a happy eternity, founded religious houses in various parts of the country, including St Albans monastery. Ethelbert was buried finally at Hereford, where a monastery had already been established over a hundred years before. Pilgrims came in great numbers to pray at his tomb, and the splendid cathedral delightfully set by the river Wye is dedicated to St Mary and St Ethelbert. Hereford Cathedral also possesses a celebrated chained library, an ancient map of the world, Mappa Mundi, and a manuscript of the Four Gospels dating from about 800. A second tomb, that of St Thomas Cantilupe, Lord Chancellor of England for a brief period in the second half of the thirteenth century, also attracted pilgrims.

We return to East Anglia for the tragic yet profoundly inspiring story of Edmund. During the Viking invasions this young king of East Anglia, who came originally from Saxony, fell into the hands of some heathen invaders. Some accounts say that he was put to death near **Thetford**, Norfolk; others relate that he was captured at **Hoxne** in Suffolk. He suffered at the hands of fighting men, being bound to a tree and used for target practice as they hurled spears or shot arrows. He had refused to deny his Christian profession in which he had been educated and nurtured from his youth; he chose martyrdom. His followers later found his body and his severed head, the latter guarded by a wolf, hence the significance of this animal in badges and emblems associated with Edmund. Just over thirty years later, in 903, his body was taken to Beodricsworth, which is known today as **Bury St Edmunds**, or St Edmund's Borough. In time a magnificent church was built; the huge abbey church and monastery, now in ruins, became the greatest and most famous in England. The present cathedral church was formerly a parish church built at a later period close by. The 'Shrine of the King, Cradle of the Law', is the title earned by this busy country town, since it was on St Edmund's Day 1214 that the barons swore at the high altar of the abbey church to make King John sign Magna Carta. But, returning to pre-Norman times, a fresh onslaught from the Vikings drove the custodians of Edmund's remains to London for safety. On their return they used the little Saxon church at **Greensted-juxta-Ongar** in Essex, unique with its split log walls, to shelter the coffin. King Canute later paid his respects at the shrine, offering a votive gold crown. There are a considerable number of churches, throughout East Anglia and elsewhere, dedicated to Edmund.

At about the same time as the monks of St Edmundsbury were laying to rest the body of Edmund, the granddaughter of King Alfred was forming a community at **Romsey**, 'an island in the marshes' bordering the beautiful trout stream, the Test. She was accompanied by several other ladies to assist in the foundation of the nunnery which was centred on a church especially built for them. Today Romsey Abbey is visited by admirers of fine architecture since this inspiring building has several rare features. The body of the much loved Earl Mountbatten of Burma now lies in this great church, not far from Broadlands where he had lived.

Through endeavour, failure, danger

In 943 a monk who was destined to leave his mark in many spheres of the Christian story — worship, evangelism, administration, craftsmanship of all kinds and above all a revitalising of monasticism—became Abbot of **Glastonbury**. His name was Dunstan and he was born locally. This celebrated prince of the church certainly deserves the epithet great, like the king who died ten years before his birth. Starting with Glastonbury, he reformed monastic life to its former ideal and this revival spread to the religious houses throughout England. At the age of fifty he was made Archbishop of Canterbury, and fourteen years later, in 973, he brought his king, Edgar the Peaceable, to coronation and enthonement as the first official King of all the English. This event, from which our present coronation rite derives, took place in the Saxon abbey church at **Bath.** This period at the end of the tenth century has been called a golden age, when there was much excellence in a wide range of art and learning. Dunstan himself was extremely talented in many pursuits from metalwork to playing the harp. In his old age at Canterbury he had a good influence on many a young scholar in the cathedral school. He died in 988 at Canterbury. Bath Abbey today, a splendid building in the Perpendicular style, the realisation of a dream, welcomes thousands in this elegant Georgian city.

There were then further devastating attacks by the Vikings. It was at about this time, in 1012, that St Alphege, Archbishop of Canterbury, was captured together with monks and nuns and taken from his cathedral city and pelted with animal bones until he died. The traditional site of his martyrdom is where the early eighteenth-century church of St Alphege stands at **Greenwich**. Four years later Canute, the Dane, became King of England together with his extensive Scandinavian empire. He was converted to the Christian faith. The little Church of the Holy Trinity at **Bosham**, set picturesquely by a creek of Chichester Harbour, is probably one of the oldest Christian sites in Sussex, where it is alleged his young daughter lies buried. He himself was buried in Winchester Cathedral, together with the Saxon kings.

Although Canute died in 1035, at the age of forty, he was a much respected king and is associated with the founding of several churches. About 1000 the Danes had destroyed the minster at **Exeter**, an ancient city which is graced today by one of England's most splendid cathedrals, predominantly in the beautiful Decorated Gothic style of the fourteenth century. Soon after becoming king, however, Canute refounded the minster and he was not the first monarch to look favourably upon this Christian outpost in the south-west dedicated to St Peter, the apostle.

Another magnificent church dedicated to this saint traces its distant origin back to Saxon England when a church was built on the Isle of Thorney in the river Thames. When jostled by crowds in Parliament Square, London, one could be excused for not knowing that this was indeed the 'terrible place' — meaning awesome — referred to in ancient writings and where a church, later **Westminster** Abbey, was founded by monks led by a certain Sebert, king of the East Saxons, over thirteen hundred years ago. To build a minster to the west of London Cathedral, that is Old St Paul's, was the decision of Edward, last of the Saxon kings, an especially religious-minded monarch, who is generally known as the Confessor for his compassionate regard for the underprivileged and his Christian devotion. He put his heart and soul into the building of the abbey church, which was in the Norman Romanesque style and stood to the north of the monastic buildings. A representation of it appears in the Bayeux Tapestry. About a week after its consecration King Edward died, on 5th January 1066. His shrine still stands behind the high altar but nothing of his church remains. This wonderful building, the coronation church, visited by millions every year, is basically the abbey realised by Henry III in the thirteenth century and it is largely in the French style.

The eventful year 1066 was a year of three kings. After Edward the Confessor's death, Harold ruled until his death on 14th October at the Battle of Hastings. William of Normandy was crowned king in the royal abbey of Westminster on Christmas Day, and almost every monarch since has been crowned here. In addition to the inspiring building itself there are innumerable features of lasting interest associated with the nation's heritage, including Poets' Corner, Henry VII's Chapel, the grave of the Unknown Warrior, the Battle of Britain Memorial Window and the tomb of David Livingstone.

William of Normandy's victory at Battle in East Sussex, a few miles inland from Hastings, was an important springboard for the Christian church and a watershed of Norman influence throughout most of Britain. In **Battle** itself there stand today a few remains of the abbey of St Martin founded by William in gratitude for victory. The high altar of the abbey church supposedly marked the actual spot at the top of Senlac Hill where the Saxon Harold was killed. A church at **Brecon** in South Wales, now Brecon Cathedral, was refounded and rebuilt by a Norman knight who fought at Hastings. It eventually became a daughter priory of Battle Abbey. Harold himself was buried in the church he had founded some years before in the Forest of Waltham, namely **Waltham Abbey** in Essex. Harold, who had experienced a cure from paralysis, had founded an abbey and Benedictine monastery at Waltham at about the same time as his brother-in-law, Edward, was following with great enthusiasm the building of his noble church at Westminster. Harold's abbey, the first Norman church in Britain, and a very fine one too, comparable in parts to Durham, was consecrated in 1060, before Westminster.

During this period the people of Scotland were not as independent as the inhabitants of Wales. The Lowlands were peopled by Saxons and Danes as on the English side of the Border. Edwin of Northumbria had founded Edwin's Burgh, Edinburgh. In 850 Kenneth MacAlpine moved his royal palace from Argyll to Scone, taking relics of St Columba from Iona to **Dunkeld.** Scotland probably had its own reformer like Dunstan in the person of Kellach of **St Andrews**, a wise and able bishop. In the eleventh century Macbeth founded monasteries and also went on a pilgrimage to Rome.

In Wales Roderic the Great, a contemporary of Alfred, had to contend with the Viking inroads as well; in his hour of victory in Anglesey he was killed. Howel the Good set down a code of laws for which he has been long remembered; he too journeyed to Rome and his assembly in **Carmarthen**, to which he summoned the Welsh princes, is a high spot in Welsh history. Llywelyn ap Seisyll, it is said, died of a broken heart when he saw the town of **St David's,** that celebrated ecclesiastical centre, going up in flames during a Viking attack.

As we have seen, Ireland, the Island of Saints, had monastic centres from which missionaries were sent to Britain and Europe. The Celtic ideal of rugged simplicity became somewhat adulterated, however, as the monasteries became too wealthy and powerful, but the *culdee* or *cele De* movement (meaning servant of God) was a reaction to this with its greater discipline and appeal to the hermit life. Learning and craftsmanship were a mark of Irish monasteries; their gifts to the world were the very beautiful and intricate manuscripts. At the very start of the eleventh century Brian Boru ruled; Ireland's greatest king, he was slain in his hour of victory against opponents who were reinforced by Norsemen, on Good Friday 1014. He had almost reached the age of ninety and, although very much a warrior, he had nevertheless been concerned about and had encouraged in a practical way churches and monasteries and the cultural side of life. He was buried in St Patrick's Cathedral, **Armagh**.

We have reached a convenient halfway point in our pilgrimage. We shall think next in terms of consolidation and also of the spread of new ideas, often with much heartsearching on the part of countless men and women in what one might call the spiritual pilgrimage, which has continued right up to our own times.

4. 1066 to 1200

The earnest looking forward

In **Edinburgh** Castle, high on its rock, one can still experience the sanctity and feel the atmosphere of a tiny Christian chapel known as St Margaret's Chapel. The pilgrim feels that here is the heart of Scotland, not just of Edinburgh, pulsating still after all the centuries, whether one is alone or simply one of the twenty or so worshippers who fill the little shrine at one time. Margaret was probably born in Hungary but when she was about twenty-two years of age she came to Scotland via the English court soon after the victory of William of Normandy. She married King Malcolm III, by whom she had six sons and two daughters. A very faithful and conscientious Christian wife and mother, she influenced Scotland very much for the good, encouraging the Christians to be more united with each other and with the church further afield in England and Europe. In 1093 Malcolm was killed in a foolish campaign into Northumberland. This tragedy broke the queen's heart, it is said, for she herself died less than a week later. Both are buried in **Dunfermline** Abbey, which they had founded, the first Benedictine house in Scotland. Robert Bruce was also buried here in 1329. Margaret's youngest son David was a great law-giver when he came to power and also a great benefactor of the church; he founded several of the great border abbeys, such as Kelso, Melrose, Jedburgh and Dryburgh. In distant Orkney St Magnus's Cathedral, **Kirkwall**, venerates Magnus, the Viking saint slain in 1117. Norman masons worked in red sandstone to produce this great church.

One used to be able to cross the river Forth by the ferry at a point where Queen Margaret crossed to her abbey at Dunfermline (hence the name Queensferry) and near the famous present-day road and rail bridges.

The following century was to see the founding, refounding or enlargement of countless monastic establishments; abbeys, priories and smaller churches throughout Britain were built in the typically Norman style embodying great daring, confidence and desire for prestige. Many great cathedral churches were of monastic origin. Some have already been mentioned and a few more are included here in a brief survey of the middle ages.

William of Normandy intended to replace all Saxon abbots and bishops with Norman ones and this he did, with one notable exception. A Midlander called Wulstan had been made Bishop of **Worcester** by Edward the Confessor in 1062. William summoned him to Westminster, a considerable trek in those days, but to a faithful and energetic pastor like Wulstan, who was used to walking about his diocese, this was probably no great trial. More of a challenge to him was his earnest belief in and desire to retain the commission received from Edward. 'I received this staff and ring from you', he declared when placing them on Edward's tomb; 'to you I return them'. The story goes that no Norman bishop present was able to move the crozier and so it was that Wulstan was the only Saxon bishop to retain his office during the Norman administration. He died nearly thirty years later. His splendid crypt beneath the majestic cathedral by the river Severn at Worcester is one of the most impressive and famous in the world. The St Wulstan Cross of modern design and workmanship has become a worthy symbol of this saintly bishop who laboured in the western midlands, where the Christian tradition dates back to St Oswald in the tenth century and to Saxon missionaries in the seventh century.

The first East Anglian cathedral church lies today beneath the waters of the North Sea, off the crumbling coast at **Dunwich** in Suffolk. At **North Elmham**, about 15 miles north-west of Norwich, there are a few remains of the Saxon cathedral which replaced it. It is, however, to the Norman bishop, Herbert de Losinga, that credit is due for the initial stages of the magnificent cathedral church of the Holy and Undivided Trinity at **Norwich,** to which the bishop's see was removed in 1094. A sad tale relates that Herbert acquired his post by a somewhat questionable method, known as simony, that is by money, but this great church is no less impressive for that and it probably represents the bishop's humble acknowledgement of his foolish un-Christian act and his willingness to make amends. Would that more Christian charity had prevailed in later centuries when town and monastery were at loggerheads. For all that, Norwich is a most awe-inspiring place and the blending of the Norman and Gothic styles in the main body of the cathedral is one of its most pleasing attributes. There is also the rare Norman apsidal east end and the bishop's throne set uniquely in the ancient position behind the high altar facing west towards clergy and people. The shrine of St William of Norwich, a little known saint elsewhere, was frequented by medieval pilgrims. The spire, second to Salisbury's masterpiece, beckons from beyond picturesque Pull's Ferry at the Watergate to the east. Norwich has much to offer the pilgrim with time to stand and stare. Nurse Edith Cavell, the Brussels heroine, is buried by the cathedral, and the birthplace of Elizabeth Fry, Quaker heroine and prison reformer, is in Magdalin Street. As at York, in the middle ages Norwich had an extraordinary number of churches, of which over thirty remain. Mother Julian of Norwich, a well known mystic, had a cell adjoining St Julian's Church. She lived and wrote of *Divine Love* in the late fourteenth century and died in 1413. She is still commemorated here.

It is a mark of the Christian way of life, indeed of the church generally, that people with the most diverse talents and seemingly inappropriate gifts have contributed greatly to the furtherance of the Christian gospel. In contrast to Mother Julian, Rahere was court jester to William Rufus and also to his successor and brother, Henry I. Henry was an able and educated monarch, although it is said not even Rahere could make him laugh after the disaster in which his only son was drowned. Rahere visited Rome and on his way home he contracted a fever from which he nearly died. He recovered, however, and returned to England, where he was granted permission to build a hospital in **London** in gratitude. The 'smooth' field beyond London's city walls was chosen for the site. Rahere's hospice, church and priory, dedicated to St Bartholomew, were the forerunners of Barts, the world-renowned hospital and church in Smithfield. In the church of St Bartholomew-the-Great, where the splendid Norman choir and transept survive, one can see Rahere's tomb. Excluding the fine Norman chapel in the Tower of London, this is the capital's oldest church, well worth a short detour to the north of St Paul's.

Pestilence and plague had led to something good being achieved. The same is true, very often, after a disaster. On 15th April 1185 a disastrous earthquake, or at least a very substantial tremor, occurred along the narrow limestone ridge where the imposing city of **Lincoln** stands today. The Norman cathedral built by Bishop Remigius, the first Norman to be given an English see, was almost completely destroyed. As happened elsewhere, the Norman policy was to remove bishoprics from quiet country settings conducive to a life of prayer and devotion to centres of government and larger townships. Thus it was that the bishop's seat was moved from secluded **Dorchester-on-Thames** to busier Lincoln. King Cynegils of Wessex had given St Birinius from Rome this pleasant site at Dorchester for his cathedral church back in 635. The present abbey is a very fine building.

After the earthquake at **Lincoln**, Hugh from Avalon in the French region of Burgundy, was sent as bishop here, the largest diocese in England. He was a saintly monk of the strict Carthusian order, named after the town of Chartreuse. Hugh was a champion of the people, a guardian of rights in an unjust world, and the appeal of this prominent twelfth-century spiritual leader, a wise choice of Henry II, has continued to this day. The Cathedral Church of St Mary, started by Hugh and finished after his death in 1200, is indeed a masterpiece of architectural splendour, probably the finest Gothic building in Britain when all things are considered. St Hugh's shrine was placed in the Angel Choir, which was begun in 1256. 150 years later the cathedral was complete, with three great spired towers and much rich ornament in glass, wood and stone. Lincoln has a feast of delights to attract the pilgrim and one such pleasure is the marvellous view towards and from the summit of the great hill on which the cathedral church rises, vast and honey-coloured, a wonderful sight from all the approach roads across the surrounding fertile farmland.

Hugh of Lincoln was still a Carthusian monk in France when one of the most momentous spiritual events in English history occurred. This was the murder of Thomas Becket, Archbishop of **Canterbury**, in his cathedral church one dark winter afternoon just after Christmas in 1170. Without Thomas the Martyr, Canterbury would still be a focal point for pilgrims, but because of his death an atmosphere of wonder, hope, peace of mind and true joy permeates the beautiful building, its city and all that it stands for. To mingle with thousands of pilgrims of diverse background and intent, to gaze in awe at the great Bell Harry Tower, to walk the vast crypt or soaring nave, all these are among the most exhilarating and rewarding experiences. To stand at the actual place of the martyrdom, silently reflecting, can be something long remembered.

During the century from about 1097 to 1189 crusades were undertaken by Christians to drive Moslems and unbelievers from the Holy Land. There are several churches of the Holy Sepulchre in England, round in style, following the pattern of the original church in Jerusalem. They can be seen at **Cambridge, Northampton, Little Maplestead** in Essex and the Temple Church in **London**. All are connected with the Knights Templar, a military order of monk knights. There were also the Knights Hospitallers and one often comes across places associated with them: the crypt of St John's, Clerkenwell, **London**, for example.

Another practice during the middle ages and a facet of church life which has been revived in recent years is that of making a pilgrimage. Indeed, one purpose of this book is to encourage the reader to visit some of the numerous shrines and holy places throughout Britain. It is hoped that the twentieth-century pilgrim will feel refreshed and renewed even though perhaps somewhat physically tired. Nowadays the pilgrim will not only wish to visit great national shrines and some of the lesser known ones, but also he or she will derive much pleasure from visiting some of the many beautiful ruins, most of which are off the beaten track in delightful and peaceful settings, and all faithfully cared for. We turn our thoughts to a few of these and to the monks and nuns who lived in them.

Although there were, and still are to a lesser extent, several different kinds of monks and nuns, nevertheless they all basically followed the Rule of Life first devised by an Italian monk long ago in the sixth century. His name was Benedict and he died at Monte Cassino, the monastery he founded in 529 near Naples. The site was badly ravaged and bombarded during the Second World War, but thankfully it is now restored. Monks following Benedict's rule are called Benedictines. As time went by new communities were started by other monks and so one finds Augustinians, Carthusians, Cistercians, and so on; some orders were very common, others less so. In England there was a period of reformation under Dunstan, as has already been mentioned; with the coming of the Normans there was further incentive to refound or establish many monasteries. In the twelfth century Stephen Harding, a monk who as a youth had been educated in **Sherborne**, Dorset, became Abbot of Citeaux, in Burgundy. The Cistercian Order (white monks after the habit they wore) was set on a sure and lasting footing by him with the help of St Bernard of Clairvaux. The Cluniac movement originated even earlier at Cluny, also in France. Both these orders represent a return to the original strict rule. Later there was an increase in the mendicant (begging) orders, the friars who, like Francis of Assisi, lived very simple lives, fairly close to other people in the towns where they preached and cared for the poor. William of **Ockham** in Surrey and Duns Scotus, a Scottish divine from **Duns**, were both prominent Franciscans, although they became somewhat worldly. The Dominican Order originated in Spain in the early thirteenth century. Dominic was a Spanish nobleman. The Carthusians, founded at La Grande Chartreuse, near Grenoble in France, lived by the single cell arrangement, a solitary life within two little rooms and a walled garden but with some communal worship; this is in contrast to all the other orders. In England this order is also known as Charterhouse.

We shall now look at a selection of monasteries. Many of our cathedrals such as Canterbury, Durham, Ely, St Albans, St Edmundsbury and Winchester were Benedictine communities. The first Cistercian monastery in England was at **Waverley** in Surrey. **Fountains** Abbey in North Yorkshire was for a while the richest Cistercian house. To approach Fountains Abbey from the east, through the secluded valley of the river Skell, near Ripon, is one of the delights of an English summer evening. The setting is incomparable for this is England's finest monastic ruin. It was at Christmastide in 1132 that monks from York, having worshipped in Ripon Minster, made their way through what must have been in those days untamed countryside. The Cistercians acquired in the years following vast tracts of land over which they pastured huge flocks of sheep. The extent of this enterprise was so great that at Grange-in-Borrowdale, nearly a hundred miles away in the Lake District, they had a grange looked after by lay brothers who tended the flocks there. **Rievaulx**, a sister abbey in the North Yorkshire moors, also in a splendid setting, was founded a year earlier. The Welsh particularly welcomed these white monks, and **Tintern** Abbey, beneath the wooded slopes of the Wye valley, has been immortalised in poetry and painting. In the beautiful Vale of Llangollen in the north lie the remains of **Valle Crucis** Abbey, founded in 1202.

Cluniac foundations can be seen in the charming Shropshire country town of **Much Wenlock** and also at **Castle Acre** in Norfolk. Little remains of the Cluniac priory at **Lewes,** in East Sussex, where today trains rumble across the site, very surprising when one considers that here was the main Cluniac house in England. There stands in this holy place a large bronze memorial to the beginning of parliamentary government in England. In 1264 the barons, led by Simon de Montfort, won a battle here against Henry III.

Mount Grace Priory in North Yorkshire is situated in moorland; here one can see a fine example of a Carthusian priory founded late in the fourteenth century. One of the little hermit cells has been restored. In the same area is **Osmotherley**, where at the market cross and stone table John Wesley, another servant of Christ in a more recent century, preached the gospel — and he was far from being a hermit! An early Methodist chapel is here too. The **London** Carthusian priory founded in 1371 became the world renowned Charterhouse School. John Wesley was a pupil at Charterhouse. St Hugh's at **Cowfold** in West Sussex is the sole Carthusian house in Britain still functioning.

5. 1200 to 1536

From glory to glory advancing

One Sunday in June 1975, on a hilltop in Wiltshire, fifteen thousand men, women and children gathered to picnic, sing hymns and listen to a powerful sermon from the Archbishop of Canterbury. The occasion was a celebration of the nine hundredth anniversary of the foundation of the diocese of **Salisbury**, with local Christian churches of varying denominations joining together for the event. The place was Old Sarum just to the north of New Sarum, modern Salisbury. It was here in 1220 that Bishop Richard Poore launched a project to build a splendid new cathedral church amidst the water meadows in the river valley. Here was a 'land flowing with milk and honey' in contrast to the bleak conditions at Old Sarum, where the military were stationed. Apart from the famous spire, Salisbury Cathedral, in the Early English Gothic style throughout, took thirty-eight years to build. It was to the shrine of St Osmund that medieval pilgrims came. Much of the middle ages can still be felt and admired today among the modern development in this beautiful city, with the contrasting greensward of the close nearby, where one can stroll and enjoy some of the fine views which compare favourably with those of any building anywhere in the world. In the same diocese at **Whitchurch Canonicorum**, Dorset, a thirteenth-century shrine still intrigues modern pilgrims. The parish church of St Candida (or Wita) and Holy Cross possesses the relics of a Saxon saint, martyred at the time of the Danish invasion. The view of the church seen through the surrounding hedgerows is particularly memorable.

The beginning of the thirteenth century was an important period in English history and in the story of human rights. For many a visit to **Runnymede,** a small island in the Thames near Windsor, is a kind of pilgrimage. Here in 1215 King John signed Magna Carta. Other memorials nearby on the wooded slopes are the John F. Kennedy Memorial and the Commonwealth Air Forces Memorial.

Wells in Somerset is one of England's smallest cities, sheltered by the lovely Mendip Hills. Here is the queen of cathedrals, still wonderfully fresh in the cream colour of the Doulting stone. In ancient times the springs of water here were known as St Andrew's wells; they still flow into the moat of the Bishop's Palace, and the cathedral itself is dedicated to Andrew, one of our Lord's first apostles. The ancient ecclesiastical buildings which surround this English Gothic cathedral have remained largely unspoiled, and they are still used today. The Vicars' Close is said to be the oldest complete street in Europe still inhabited after six hundred years. The west front of the cathedral, England's finest, has a stupendous display of statues, of which there were originally nearly four hundred. Among the saints, apostles and monarchs represented are many mentioned in this book. Among the unknown statues perhaps there is one to the next saint to be considered, namely St Richard, the much loved Bishop of Chichester.

Richard was a Worcestershire man. He studied at Oxford, where he befriended Edmund Rich of Abingdon, a notable scholar and treasurer of Salisbury Cathedral when that masterpiece was taking shape in the 1220s. Edmund Rich later became Archbishop of Canterbury and Richard of **Chichester** was his right-hand man. Though he walked with kings, Richard never lost the common touch, and in West Sussex at the beautiful cathedral in Chichester, where his shrine once attracted countless pilgrims, he is remembered most for his appeal to the average English person, 'plain and good like bread; a kind, humble, steadfast, cheerful man' in the words of Dorothy L. Sayers. Richard gave us an often quoted prayer that we may 'know more clearly, love more dearly, and follow more nearly.' During a preaching tour, Richard died at **Dover** within a day or so of dedicating a little chapel to Edmund, his colleague. This can still be seen in the vicinity of the Maison Dieu buildings, the present town hall, a guest house in the thirteenth century. It is, however, in Chichester Cathedral that one experiences something of what Bishop Richard meant to the people of Sussex. The numerous modern works of art in this cathedral, which is basically Norman and Early English, are also imaginative and of a high calibre.

In great churches like Chichester Cathedral one is able to appreciate great art from many centuries. Indeed great works of art are for all time and are in a sense timeless. Britain has an especially rich heritage in its churches. There are many thousands of parish churches of medieval origin, and some that are even earlier, and one aspect of modern pilgrimage is the enjoyment of beautiful things. In the middle ages the parish church with its Christian festivals and holy days (holidays) was very much the centre of life.

'I thank my God and ever shall, it is the sheep hath paid for all' is a prayer of thanksgiving offered by a rich Cotswold merchant of the middle ages. Great wealth was earned in the wool trade and magnificent churches rose at the expense of such men who had made fortunes in this way. Coupled with this was much civic and family pride. Many a village or country town in parts of East Anglia and the Cotswolds is crowned with an impressive 'wool church' — **Lavenham, Long Melford, Northleach** and **Cirencester**, to name but four.

One educational aspect of medieval life was the custom of performing miracle or mystery plays. These were usually performed by the trade guilds in the open air and mostly concerned religious subjects. The plays were grouped in cycles. The York Cycle contains forty-eight plays. Other play cycles include those of Chester, Coventry, Lincoln and Wakefield. Carpenters would find the story of Noah's ark appropriate to perform. The goldsmiths at York were the Wise Men. In recent years there has been a revival of these plays and holiday crowds watch performances in the ruins adjacent to the modern cathedral at Coventry. The abbey at **Chester** produced the earliest of its mystery plays in the fourteenth century. A certain Henry Francis, one of the monks, was the medieval impresario there. Here, too, was the shrine of a Saxon princess, St Werburgh. The abbey church, a cathedral since 1541, is especially noted for its surrounding monastic buildings and, within the cathedral church itself, the exquisite wood carving of the stalls, a medieval masterpiece not to be missed.

Plays recounting the life, death and resurrection of Christ were performed in Cornish open-air theatres. Such a *plan-an-Guare* (playing place) can be seen at **St Just-in-Penwith**. John and Charles Wesley often stopped on their travels to preach here. In some places fairs were another preoccupation: St Giles Fair at Winchester under the bishop's watchful eye and direction and the one at Stourbridge near Cambridge were two of the most famous.

Towards the end of the thirteenth century Edward I brought the Stone of Scone, on which Scottish kings were crowned, from Scotland to Westminster Abbey. His wife, Eleanor of Castile, had died at Lincoln in 1290. Of the tall elaborate stone crosses set up to mark where her coffin rested on its journey south, only four

1. Pilgrims at St Albans Cathedral, Hertfordshire, which stands on the site of the execution of Britain's first Christian martyr, Alban, in 209.

2. *Pilgrims amongst the ruins of Glastonbury Abbey, Somerset, a holy place connected with St Joseph of Arimathea and the reputed burial place of King Arthur.*

3. St Martin's church at Canterbury, Kent, was where Queen Bertha worshipped before St Augustine's mission. The cathedral can be seen in the distance.

4. Stonor Park in Oxfordshire, seat of the Camoys family, which remained steadfast in the Catholic faith throughout the Reformation, giving shelter to Catholic priests, including the subsequently martyred Edmund Campion.

5. The ruins of Rievaulx Abbey in the North Yorkshire Moors, founded by the Cistercians in 1131.
6. The historic church of Winchelsea in East Sussex. It was in this churchyard that John Wesley preached his last open-air sermon.

7. St David's Cathedral, Dyfed, the cradle of Christianity in Wales, was founded in the sixth century during the lifetime of the saint, who was born nearby.

8. *(Left) This tall cross near Pegwell Bay, Kent, marks the spot where St Augustine and his monks came ashore in 597. It is now half a mile inland.*

9. *(Right) This monument on Nibley Knoll, in the Cotswolds of southern Gloucestershire, commemorates William Tyndale, who translated the Bible into English and was martyred in 1536.*

10. (Left) In Geddington, Northamptonshire, stands one of the Eleanor crosses erected by King Edward I to mark the resting places of the coffin of his queen, Eleanor, on its way from Lincoln, where she died, to London.

11. (Right) The statue of Isaac Watts, called the Father of English hymns, in Southampton, the city of his birth.

12. Whitby Abbey, North Yorkshire, was the scene in 664 of the great synod at which Christians of the northern, Celtic church met representatives of the Roman church of southern England.

13. St Peter's church, Monkwearmouth, Tyne and Wear. The tower survives from the church of the abbey where Bede was taken as a young orphan.

14. Sherborne Abbey, Dorset. In Anglo-Saxon times Sherborne was the centre of a bishopric, and St Aldhelm was the first bishop.

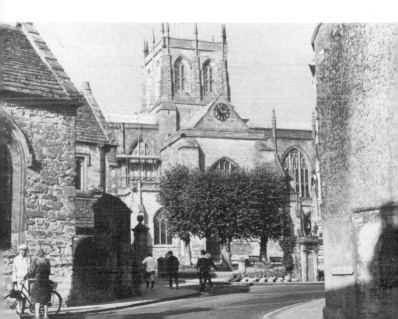

15. The spire of Salisbury Cathedral, Wiltshire, seen from Harnham Mill. It was in 1220 that Bishop Poore began to build the cathedral here among the water meadows, abandoning the bleak site at Old Sarum.

16. The Slipper Chapel at Houghton St Giles, Norfolk. Here pilgrims on their way to the shrine of the Virgin Mary at nearby Little Walsingham would remove their shoes and proceed barefoot.

17. The Carmelite nunnery and church at Lanherne, Cornwall, where the Roman Catholic priest Cuthbert Mayne ministered in Elizabeth I's reign. He was arrested and executed at Launceston.

18. The cloisters of Canterbury Cathedral, mother church of the Church of England.

19. The Mayflower Stone at Plymouth commemorates the Pilgrim Fathers, who finally embarked here on their way to New England in 1620.

20. The Moot Hall at Elstow near Bedford. In this village John Bunyan, author of 'The Pilgrim's Progress', was born and baptised.
21. In 1652, on Pendle Hill in Lancashire, George Fox experienced a vision which led him to found the Quaker movement.

22. One of the oldest and most attractive Friends' meeting houses is at Jordans, Buckinghamshire. William Penn is buried in the graveyard.
23. Aylesford Friary, Kent, was re-established in 1949, seven hundred years after its original foundation, and it is much visited by Christians of different denominations.

24. The shrine of St Birinius in Dorchester Abbey, Oxfordshire. King Cynegils of Wessex gave Birinius this site for his cathedral in 635, but the Normans moved the bishopric to Lincoln.

25. *The Pilgrims' Way near Compton, Surrey. This ancient trackway was used by pilgrims on their way to Canterbury, and the North Downs Way, a modern long-distance footpath, follows it for much of its course.*

remain, at **Northampton, Geddington, Waltham Cross** and **Charing Cross** (not the original). Edward's son, who became Edward II when his father died in 1307, was too much of a waster, handsome, but weak and foolish. He failed in his campaigns in Scotland, suffering defeat at Bannockburn in 1314. He also suffered an ignoble death in **Berkeley** Castle thirteen years later. The Abbot of **Gloucester** Abbey (a cathedral church only since 1541) arranged an elaborate burial service in the abbey church. It is rather astonishing that pilgrims came in vast numbers to venerate such an unworthy monarch, but the monks did not complain since their rather sombre Norman building was transformed with the splendid brightness and sense of space afforded by the new choir, paid for by the pilgrims' offerings. In consequence there is at Gloucester Cathedral one of the noblest and largest windows in the world. The pinnacled tomb of the king with its lovely alabaster effigy stands near a poignant reminder of other evil deeds, namely the cross carved by Colonel Carne VC of the Gloucestershire Regiment whilst in solitary confinement as a prisoner of war in Korea.

Arise, O Morning Star

The printed word is something taken very much for granted nowadays but until the closing years of the middle ages the art of printing was virtually unknown. Manuscripts, handwritten documents and books were exceedingly precious. A departure from the normal 'religious' works such as those referred to earlier — Bede's *History* and various gospels — was a great work of scientific findings written by a Franciscan friar, Roger Bacon. His *Opus Majus* is generally regarded as the greatest work of its kind. Born at Ilchester in Somerset, he went to Oxford. At **Sunningwell** to the south-west, near Abingdon, the tower of the village church was the scene of some of his experiments; pilgrims will find this intriguing. Roger was a pupil of the Suffolk-born Bishop of Lincoln, the celebrated Grosseteste, and he lived from 1214 to 1293.

Two outstanding literary works of the fourteenth century deserve mention here. Geoffrey Chaucer wrote poetry and later the immortal *Canterbury Tales*, stories related by pilgrims 'cantering' to Canterbury. The other great work was the translation of the Holy Bible into English by John Wyclif. He became master of Balliol College, Oxford, and was outspoken in his criticism of the leaders of the Church. He became priest-in-charge of the parish of **Lutterworth,** in Leicestershire, where there is a memorial to him in St Mary's Church. Here, in what is now a large village, this earnest religious reformer worked for well over fifteen years on the translation. Some years after his death his writings were condemned, his body was disinterred and after burning the ashes were thrown into the river Swift. Wyclif lived from 1320 to 1384 and is known as the 'Morning Star of the English Reformation'. His bible men or poor priests, sent out into the highways and byways of England, were known as Lollards and were later hunted down and persecuted.

The fourteenth century was the age of chivalry, a code of living for the knights of Europe, a code of ideals which the Church could not fail to encourage; it was a time of great advances in architecture, as most cathedral and parish churches testify. The central tower at **Ely**, the unique octagon and lantern, is an example. It is the only Gothic dome, a *tour de force*, the effect of which is amazing. **Exeter** Cathedral is England's finest decorated Gothic cathedral. However, during this century there were three devastating setbacks. The Black Death bubonic plague ravaged Europe and caused the death of a very large number of the population of Britain in the 1340s. Forty years later came the Peasants' Revolt against restrictive legislation and poor conditions. Amidst all this was the start of the Hundred Years War with France. One will often find, in churches of all kinds, monuments and features connected with these events. Edward the Black Prince, hero of Crecy and Poitiers, died a slow death at the age of forty-six. His effigy at **Canterbury** is one of the most notable monuments.

In the following century England was ravaged by the Wars of the Roses. The magnificent Norman and Gothic abbey at **Tewkesbury**, refounded in 1087, of cathedral-like proportions, hallowed and welcoming, shelters beneath its fine Norman tower (the largest in existence) the grave of seventeen-year-old Edward, Prince of Wales, who was killed at the Battle of Tewkesbury in 1471. This splendid abbey church, its monastic buildings mostly now destroyed, has a memorable setting in this attractive country town where the rivers Avon and Severn meet.

Also in Gloucestershire, at ancient **Winchcombe** north-east of Cheltenham are the few remains of the once great monastery where the martyr king Kenelm was honoured. A short distance away are the ruins of **Hayles** Abbey (or Hailes), once famous for the relic of the Holy Blood of Christ.

The year 1471 was doubly tragic, for then also the deposed king, Henry VI, died, presumed murdered, in the Tower of London. A man of deep religious conviction, at the age of twenty he founded Eton College and King's College, **Cambridge**. Various setbacks caused by the Wars of the Roses delayed work on the chapel at King's College, but the result is a truly magnificent building in the late Gothic style called Perpendicular and noted for its superb fan vault; Henry VII's Chapel in Westminster Abbey is another wonderful architectural achievement. In 1484 holy King Henry VI was laid to rest finally at the newly built St George's Chapel at

Windsor Castle. The Order of the Garter founded by Edward III, who was 'every thing a king should be', had its own chapel on the site prior to the rebuilding. The Knights of the Garter still display their banners here. The tomb of King Henry is marked by a slab. Lilies from Eton and King's adorn his grave every year on the anniversaries of his birth, 6th December, and death, 21st May.

It may surprise some people to learn that King Henry VIII went on a pilgrimage to one of the most celebrated shrines in all England, a shrine which most people still associate with pilgrimage and varying depths of devotion right up to the present. **Walsingham**, England's Nazareth, traces its origins back to the early twelfth century. A widow of Little Walsingham had a vision of the Virgin Mary's home in Nazareth, which she was urged to have built in replica in Norfolk. There were several routes to this shrine, one of which passed via the pilgrims' port of **King's Lynn**. The late fifteenth-century Chapel of the Red Mount at King's Lynn is the finest wayside pilgrims' chapel in England; it is sometimes called St Mary-on-the-Hill. Another route, that from London, passed along the ancient Icknield Way to Fakenham. This route also had its stopping places for pilgrims, such as **Castle Acre** Priory on the old Peddars' Way. King Henry travelled the last mile or so on foot, his mind burdened, it is said, with prayer for his infant son born of Catharine. At the Slipper Chapel at **Houghton St Giles** it was the custom to remove one's shoes. The routes from the east and north Norfolk coasts included visits to **Bromholm,** where a portion of the true cross or Holy Rood could be reverenced, and **Binham** Priory, much nearer to Walsingham, and where today the nave is in use. It was in 1931 that Anglo Catholics started restoration work; in due course the Roman Catholics came back as well. For many twentieth-century pilgrims the annual pilgrimage to Walsingham is a highlight of the Christian year.

We end this brief survey of the Christian faith in the middle ages with the prayer of a remarkable man. A few miles south-east of Berkeley Castle and in the Gloucestershire Cotswolds a monument was raised on **Nibley Knoll** in honour of William Tyndale, a man whose life story is as spine-chilling as that of any modern spy. A statue in London also recalls this great man's achievement. It can be seen on the Victoria Embankment in the gardens beyond Horse Guards Avenue. 'If God spares my life, before many years I will cause a boy who drives the plough to know the Bible better than you do', proclaimed Tyndale to a scholar at Oxford. It was this deep conviction that drove him to work tirelessly (and dangerously) on a fresh translation of the Holy Bible against much opposition, which finally caused him to flee the country. Copies of his translation were smuggled into England from the Continent but they were burned in public at St Paul's in London. Many copies of both the Old and the New Testaments did, however, reach the people. William was eventually betrayed, tried and tortured and burnt near Brussels. The year was 1536, the day 6th October. Aged fifty-two, his dying prayer was: 'O Lord, open the eyes of the King of England'.

6. 1536 to 1600

A safe stronghold our God is still

William Tyndale's prayer was answered within three years and in due course it was decreed that a copy of the Bible should be placed in every church and it was usually chained. This symbolises a growing awareness of the New Learning and personal search for truth which epitomised the years ahead, the years of the Renaissance and Reformation. Critics of the Church pointed out that its leaders especially were failing to live in the true spirit of the Gospel. A prime example was Cardinal Thomas Wolsey, Henry VIII's chaplain, who had a palace built at Hampton Court. Dismissed and disgraced by the king, Thomas died at Leicester Abbey in 1530.

With the momentous advance occasioned by the invention of printing with movable type, promoted in England by William Caxton, ideas were being propagated more easily, not least the very word of Christ himself in a language the ordinary folk could understand. In 1536, the year of Tyndale's death, there died also the Dutch scholar Desiderius Erasmus, who had paid several visits to England and had befriended Dean Colet of St Paul's and Sir Thomas More. It is often jokingly said that 'Erasmus laid the egg which Luther hatched' and this Luther had done on All Saints Day in 1517, when he nailed his theses to the church door at Wittenberg.

The priory church of St Peter in **Dunstable,** the fine remnant of an early twelfth-century Augustine priory, was the setting for the declaration of the annulment of the marriage of Henry VIII with Catharine of Aragon. Henry opposed the Pope on political grounds and in 1534 the Act of Supremacy made the King head of the English Church. The following year both Sir Thomas More (the 'Man for All Seasons', renowned for his book *Utopia* and a former Lord Chancellor) and St John Fisher, Bishop of Rochester, opposed the King and suffered martyrdom in consequence. Sir Thomas was beheaded on Tower Hill, 'the King's good servant but God's first'. His head was later taken to the Church of St Dunstan in **Canterbury,** the church at which, nearly four hundred years before, Henry II had dismounted to walk to the cathedral in penitence for Thomas Becket's death.

A lawyer, Thomas Cromwell, Earl of Essex, attended to the

Dissolution of the Monasteries, of which there were well over six hundred in England alone. In 1536 four hundred of the smaller houses were closed. Within three years the larger establishments met the same fate. Many of these religious houses had been in decline for some time; moreover, many had ceased to be shining examples of godly living. In all these events it is well to remember that Henry remained a Catholic at heart. Indeed, he persecuted followers of the protesting Luther. In Yorkshire, where there were over 150 monasteries, and in Lincolnshire the loss of these religious houses was felt the most. A public demonstration against the closure, the Pilgrimage of Grace, resulted in the death of the ringleaders; in all over two hundred people were killed.

A chantry (from the French *chanter*, to sing) was a chapel within a church especially endowed so that a priest could say mass therein for the benefactor's soul after his death. One of the most exquisite chantry chapels is to be seen in **Christchurch** Priory in Dorset. It is associated with Margaret, Countess of Salisbury, whose son became Cardinal Pole. When in her seventies, Margaret was executed at the Tower of London, the reason being that both she and her son were staunch Catholics, and she had criticised Henry VIII's actions. This fine priory church at the mouth of the Avon and Stour rivers has an impressive Norman nave arcade. The intriguing miraculous beam is at the heart of a beautiful early medieval legend, associated with Christ and this church — Christchurch. The collection of chantries in **Winchester** Cathedral forms one of that great church's treasured features. Two early sixteenth-century bishops, Richard Fox and Stephen Gardiner, rest in chantries here, just beyond the high altar, while Bishop William of Wykeham's chantry is in the Perpendicular Gothic nave, a splendid nave indeed, arising out of the ingenious reconstruction and unique encasing of the Norman building. As a lad William had often stood nearby and this glorious nave is his achievement and that of his master mason, William Wynford.

On Whit Sunday 1549 Archbishop Cranmer's new Prayer Book was introduced. Eleven-year-old Edward VI was king at the time. The little Devon village of **Sampford Courtenay**, just west of Exeter, seems remote enough from the central corridors of power, yet it was the scene of a rebellion against the 'party games' style of the new services. The mass-loving western men, Cornishmen in particular, marched and died for the cause of retaining the old liturgy. Humphrey Arundell, a celebrated Catholic, campaigned from the ancient site of **St Michael's Mount,** probably the most famous place of pilgrimage in the far western peninsula. It is still a very beautiful place, an impressive and memorable counterpart to the much grander Mont St Michel across the Channel off the Normandy coast. At the time of the Prayer Book rebellion the city of **Exeter** was under siege for a month, until the new Protestant regime won the day. At St Thomas's church the body of the vicar, still in vestments, was left hanging from the tower for four years.

The reign of Mary was particularly marred by gruesome persecution, arising out of her desire to champion the Roman Catholic cause. Bishop Hooper was burned at **Gloucester,** Bishop Taylor at **Lincoln,** and Bishop Ferrar at **St Davids.** Archbishop Cranmer and Bishops Latimer and Ridley went heroically to the flames as well, and the Martyrs' Memorial in **Oxford** commemorates their stand. Latimer's famous words to Master Ridley ('Play the man. We shall this day light such a candle, by God's grace, in England as I trust shall never be put out.') are a reminder that persecution was to strengthen the Protestant cause. On the wall of St Bartholomew's Hospital at Smithfield, **London,** memorials recall other Protestant martyrs — there were nearly three hundred in all, many of them ordinary folk — and also Sir William Wallace, the Scottish hero whose death in 1305 inflamed nationalism north of the border more and more.

There were Roman Catholic martyrs too, however. In Elizabeth I's reign much cloak and dagger intrigue, plot and counterplot prevailed. To argue against and oppose the Anglican Church was a treasonable offence. Edmund Campion and Robert Parsons, Jesuit missionaries of the Counter Reformation, were trained on the Continent. Cuthbert Mayne returned from Douai to Cornwall and ministered in secret at **Lanherne** and at Golden, where he was arrested in 1577. He was later tried and executed at **Launceston,** where his shrine can be seen at the Roman Catholic Church of the English Martyrs. At Lanherne itself, in a delightful rural setting, is Cornwall's most notable Roman Catholic centre, the oldest Carmel in England; the nuns here are custodians of Blessed Cuthbert Mayne's skull. It is said that hiding places known as priests' holes exist hereabouts. Many old **houses all over Britain possess such places of refuge for persecuted** priests, secret and ingeniously hidden.

It is hard for us today to equate a love of God, brotherhood and true devotion for Christ with the actions of Christians on both sides in those sad, tragic days. Mary, for instance, was not a cruel person by nature but as Queen she believed, along with many others, that it was better for heretics to be disposed of than that they should live in mortal sin. Elizabeth, it is said, ordered a copy of John Foxe's *Book of Martyrs* to be placed in churches for all to see, and this in itself hardly poured oil on troubled waters but rather fanned hatred of fellow Christians of a different persuasion.

Scotland experienced the Reformation in a very profound way, more so, it is argued, than any other country. On 29th February 1528, outside the College of St Salvator at **St Andrews,** the dedicated preacher Patrick Hamilton was burned for heresy. Some years later George Wishart suffered the same fate in the same place. John Knox, having served as a galley slave in a French ship and having on release studied at Geneva at the feet of the great exponent of biblical teaching, John Calvin, returned in 1559 to Scotland and preached Reformation in earnest. His first Reformation sermon was delivered at St Andrew's Castle. He celebrated the first communion according to the new rite at **Mid Calder House,** south-west of Edinburgh. The house known as John Knox House, where relics of his life and time may be seen, stands in the Royal Mile in **Edinburgh,** just below the celebrated Carrubers Close Mission of more recent times, where the Word of God is faithfully proclaimed.

John Knox also had a likable and gentle trait to his fiery nature. Queen Elizabeth of England finally made an alliance with Protestant Scotland. A statement of Reformation doctrine and a book of disipline were drawn up. A kirk and a school in every parish was Knox's aim. Scotland now had a Reformed Church and it was at this point that Mary, Queen of Scots, aged eighteen, returned from France. Knox was invited to a friendly meeting with the young queen at Loch Leven Castle. She had private celebrations of the Catholic mass in the Palace of Holyrood in Edinburgh and this displeased John Knox, and he said so publicly in sermons. Life did not go well for the sad queen. Her son, James, was crowned at Stirling after her forced abdication. After enduring a sixty-mile nonstop ride on horseback, she spent her last night in Scotland at **Dundrennan** Abbey. The year was 1568. The following day she crossed into England, where her cousin, Queen Elizabeth, confined her for nearly twenty years. Fearing a Catholic plot and having intercepted incriminating letters, Elizabeth signed Mary's death warrant with much regret. As one approaches **Fotheringhay** in Northamptonshire, its octagonal-towered church beautifully reflected in the gentle flow of the river Nene, one hardly associates this village with the death of a queen, and yet it was here, in a castle of which only a mound remains, that Mary was executed on 8th February 1587. 'I forgive you with all my heart,' she said. The Dean of Peterborough Cathedral, where she was originally buried, tried to convert her away from the Catholic faith, but to no avail. The following year came Catholic Spain's attempt, in the form of the Great Armada, to reconvert England, but that also proved a complete failure. 'God blew and they were scattered,' was the cry of victory.

7. 1600 to 1700

To be a pilgrim . . .

At midnight on 26th March 1603 England and Scotland became united under a Scottish king, when James VI, Mary's son, became also James I of England. Both Puritans and Catholics, at opposite extremes of religious belief, hoped for favours but these were not forthcoming — witness the Catholic-inspired Gunpowder Plot.

The Puritans wished to 'purify the Church'; they sought a return to simple New Testament Christianity. Elizabeth 'made no windows into men's souls . . . think what you wish but keep quiet about it . . .' At **Gainsborough** in Lincolnshire one group of Puritans met regularly together. This group was later centred on the little village of **Scrooby** in Nottinghamshire on the Great North Road. William Brewster, a founder member of the Pilgrim Fathers, is remembered here where he was born. Other leaders were John Robinson, once an Anglican, and William Bradford, who became governor of a colony in the New World. Worship took place in secret at the Manor House; this is where independency or congregationalism had its birth. An escape route to Holland and thence to America was through **Boston** in Lincolnshire. The tower of St Botolph's Church here in Botolph's town (Botolph was a Saxon monk) is known as the Stump and it is justly famous the world over, being 272½ feet (83 m) in height. The interior of the church is also most rewarding with its fine roof and carved stalls. Cells in the Guildhall were where the Pilgrim Fathers were held in custody. John Cotton, the celebrated Puritan vicar here, sailed to Boston, Massachusetts. On 4th July every year the Stars and Stripes can be seen flying above Boston's river Witham and the flat landscape towards the sea. The Pilgrim Fathers sailed from **Southampton** in August 1620. Their memorial near the Westgate takes the form of a tall inscribed pillar, surmounted by a model of the *Mayflower*. It was necessary for the Pilgrims to put in at **Plymouth** and therefore at the Barbican here there is the Mayflower Stone set into the pavement, and also one is shown the steps from which the Pilgrims finally embarked. (Martyrs of a later century are also recalled to mind here.) Bayards Cove in **Dartmouth** also has a monument commemorating the Pilgrim Fathers. In Southwark, **London,** the Pilgrim Fathers' Memorial Church, the oldest Congregational church, built in 1616, was last rebuilt in 1956. Several places proudly recall their connection with the Pilgrims; people with this American connection in mind will find many references elsewhere.

King James held an important conference at **Hampton Court** in January 1604 at which one suggestion was the production of an entirely new authorised translation of the Bible. It was pointed out that there were already too many versions — Tyndale's, Miles

Coverdale's, and so on. For this reason the famous *Authorised Version,* loved and disliked today, was born. The idea had already been put forward in 1601 at **Burntisland** in Fife in Scotland, on the occasion of the General Assembly of the Church there. King James himself was also present on that occasion. Work on the translation took several years and its public appearance was in 1611.

The Puritans in Ireland were given a freer hand and the Protestant bishop, James Ussher, who set down the chronology of the biblical events, was made Primate of the Irish Church. In Wales a very worthy bishop of the early seventeenth century is commemorated at the cathedral church at **St Asaph.** He is William Morgan, who with the assistance of a few colleagues translated the scriptures into Welsh. There is a memorial outside and he is buried inside this cathedral. St Asaph is reputedly the smallest cathedral in England and Wales, and it is one of the most ancient, dating from the sixth century, when St Kentigern (alias Mungo, patron saint of Glasgow), placed Asaph in charge here.

The great city of **Glasgow** has for its cathedral one of the grandest and most satisfying medieval buildings in Scotland, especially the crypt. St Mungo was buried here in 603. The founder of the Catholic Apostolic Church, Edward Irving, is buried here too; he is also associated with Henry Drummond at Albury in Surrey in the nineteenth century — the Irvingites. In this crypt in Glasgow Cathedral the well nearby takes one back, in spirit at least, to the times fourteen centuries ago when all around was forest. Covenanters are also remembered here. In 1638 the Great Assembly met in the cathedral and the Presbyterian Church of Scotland was officially proclaimed; twenty-three years later the episcopacy was restored. The Roman Catholic priest, John Ogilvie, was martyred, aged thirty-five, at Glasgow Cross for defending the Pope's spiritual supremacy. In 1976 this martyr was canonised for his apparent intercession on behalf of a man who in the 1970s was miraculously healed from terminal cancer. Also in 1638 Greyfriars Church in **Edinburgh** was the scene of the signing of the National Covenant, against Anglicanisation of the Scottish Church.

Although the dissenting Christians everywhere were forced to become the 'underground church', as happens in some places even today, there are, nonetheless, chapels and meeting places which date from these early days of Nonconformity. **Tewkesbury** has a very early Baptist chapel and at **Walpole** in Suffolk is an early seventeenth-century meeting house, the Congregational Chapel.

Civil War broke out in 1642 and lasted for four years, ending with Charles I's defeat. From 1643, however, until 1649 learned scholars from the universities at Oxford and Cambridge met to formulate a Confession of Faith, to be the basis of a united church in Britain. About a month before this celebrated Assembly of Divines at Westminster had completed its debate, Charles had been condemned to death. Together with his Archbishop, William Laud, Charles had believed in the Divine Right of Kings and indeed of the episcopacy. There was bound to be a clash of opinion, considering the religious climate of the time. In the early stages of the Civil War the Parliamentary forces under Cromwell were somewhat taken aback and disheartened by John Hampden's death, at the Battle of **Chalgrove** Field in Oxfordshire. John Hampden had once refused to pay the King's unlawful Ship Money. Later the Scots, who had been disgruntled and much angered by the King's attitude, joined forces with the English Parliamentary army. At one o'clock in the afternoon of 30th January 1649, Charles walked through a window of the Banqueting House in **Whitehall** before a vast crowd and nobly submitted his head to the axe. A fine equestrian statue of Charles stands in Whitehall today, and on the anniversary of his death special tributes are paid and prayers said by Christians who believe he was a martyr.

Oliver Cromwell was profoundly earnest in his devotion to what he believed was the will of God. As a Puritan he won the hearts of his men, who believed God was fighting for them against frivolity, corruption, wickedness and idolatry in the Church. For this reason so much beauty in art and architecture, Britain's precious heritage, was wantonly destroyed. One need look no further than **Ely** Cathedral Lady Chapel, within a stone's throw of where Cromwell lived for a time. His campaign in Ireland was incredibly severe and much resentment remains to this day.

After about eleven years came the Restoration of the monarchy with Charles II, who had leanings towards the Roman Catholic Church, but surprisingly there was little yielding to the latter, or indeed to Nonconformists.

He who would valiant be

'As I walked through the wilderness of this world, I lighted on a certain place . . . to sleep; and as I slept, I dreamed a dream.' So begins one of the greatest pieces of writing in the world, so familiar and yet, like the Holy Bible, to which it comes a close second in the realm of Christian literature, so little known. *The Pilgrim's Progress* was started by John Bunyan, son of a travelling tinker, whilst serving a second sentence in the old gaol on **Bedford** bridge in 1676. His first prison sentence lasted twelve years from 1660 to 1672; his crime was preaching in and around Bedford. Relics of his life and times may be seen at Bunyan Meeting House in Bedford, whilst a notable statue of this early Baptist preacher graces St Peter's Green. John was baptised in the fine medieval church at neighbouring **Elstow** where he was born and where the old Moot Hall, now a museum, still stands. Did John perhaps experience conversion whilst playing on the green here? He has other writings to his credit, such as *The Holy War* and *Grace Abounding.* He is buried in **Bunhill Fields** in London, to the north-east of the Barbican development, opposite Wesley's Chapel.

From Bunyan's masterpiece we turn to one of more recent times, but one which takes the pilgrim back to the early years of the seventeenth century and to a place 'where prayer has been valid'. 'If you come this way, taking the route you would be likely to take' . . . T. S. Eliot brings us to **Little Gidding** in Cambridgeshire in this quotation from *The Four Quartets.* The little church here has a delightful interior furnished like a college chapel. To this holy place in peaceful countryside the English theologian, Nicholas Ferrar, came with his mother and other relatives in 1625. They sought quiet seclusion for a life of contemplation and kindly deeds. Nicholas died twelve years later aged forty-five. He outlived by about four years an equally contemplative soul and close friend, George Herbert, who was born into a well-to-do family in Montgomery in Wales. At the time of his death he was a humble country parson at **Bemerton** near Salisbury, where he ministered with his wife, Jane, for just three years. Every week he went to choral services in Salisbury Cathedral, the spire of which still beckons one as it did this man known as the poet laureate of the Anglican Church. As one walks in the area of the water meadows of the river Nadder, between Bemerton and the cathedral city, one can easily recall George Herbert's paraphrase of Psalm 23, or his hymn 'Let all the world in every corner sing, my God and King'. St Andrew's, Bemerton, shelters his body. Nicholas Ferrar's grave at Little Gidding has no name.

A few miles north-east of Whalley's ruined Cistercian abbey, in Lancashire, rises **Pendle Hill.** George Fox, as a man of twenty-eight, who had had a deep experience of the inner light of Christ, climbed over 1800 feet (550 m) to its summit one day in 1652. There, through the misty heights, he had a vision 'of people to be gathered to the Lord'. The experience led him to preach more and more in the open air and to found the Quaker Movement. He was born at **Fenny Drayton** in Leicestershire and grew to despise traditional churches, which he called 'steeple houses'.

The previous year in **Lichfield,** the city of the three spires, he had declared, whilst walking prophet-like up and down barefooted, 'Woe unto the city of Lichfield'. Within a few years there were fifty thousand Quakers, mockingly so nicknamed for their trembling emotion as they urged people, judges and peasants alike, to tremble in the fear of the Lord. They increased in number very fast and called themselves the Society of Friends; hundreds were imprisoned as indeed was George Fox himself. **Swarthmore Hall** in the English Lake District was his Quaker headquarters and it remains a centre to this day. In true Reformation fashion they stressed the importance of the individual's relationship with God. Today they are much respected for their non-violence and for their positive work in alleviating suffering and eradicating social and political evils.

The name of another celebrated Quaker, also persecuted in his youth, lives on in Pennsylvania, United States, and his city of brotherly love, Philadelphia. He is William Penn, who is buried at **Jordans,** Buckinghamshire, in the graveyard by the attractively simple Friends' Meeting House. This lovely countryside is a delight, remote in the beech-clad Chiltern Hills. The Mayflower Barn at a nearby farm, now a hostel, possesses timbers, it is said, from the famous ship of that name. The church in the Chiltern village of **Penn** also has many Penn family associations. Understandably, Quaker places of worship are quite unpretentious. One of the oldest has the surprising name of Blue Idol; it is an old converted farmhouse near **Coolham,** West Sussex, and this was frequented by William Penn. In 1677 George Fox preached at the new **Brigg Flatts** Meeting House in Cumbria. At the other end of the country one of the most memorable and cottage-like, with an enchanting name, is the thatched meeting house at **Come-to-Good,** in a Cornish coastal coomb near Feock, south-west of Truro.

The year 1665 is remembered for the notorious London plague, which decimated the population and which called forth from the Puritans the declaration that the Almighty was punishing the sinful city; the Commonwealth of Oliver Cromwell had now passed and Restoration under a merry monarch had been in full swing for five years already, much to the distress of the Nonconformist dissenters. John Milton, an admirer of Cromwell, was already fifty-seven years old and becoming blind when he arrived at the village of **Chalfont St Giles,** Buckinghamshire. Today his cottage is a museum and to all who are interested in literature, and especially poetry, this is an evocative place of pilgrimage. It was here that his epic *Paradise Lost* was completed and *Paradise Regained* was written at the suggestion of John's Quaker friend, Ellwood. Writing was the main art-form open to Puritans, it must be remembered, since even church music and architecture were ungodly pleasures in their eyes.

Under Catholic James II Scottish Covenanters and English bishops feared the return of the old Catholic religion. But James was overthrown, and the theory of Divine Right was no more. The Toleration Act of 1689 allowed Nonconformists greater freedom. Over a hundred years later came the Catholic Relief Act giving freedom of education and worship to Roman Catholics, and in 1829 the Catholic Emancipation Act was passed. In the eighteenth century and after, almost one thousand new places of worship were built by the Nonconformists. As four hundred thousand Huguenot refugees fled from France, many of whom were welcomed and allowed to settle in Britain, toleration was to grow.

8. 1700 to 1800

O for a thousand tongues to sing

Thomas Ken was one of seven bishops who saved England, since he refused to take the oath to William and Mary, and in consequence he suffered imprisonment in the Tower of London and also the loss of his bishopric, that of Bath and Wells. He had been present at the death of Charles II and died himself at **Longleat** House in 1711. The library in this splendid house still contains his wonderful collection of books. Recalling his hymn 'Awake my soul and with the sun', his canopied grave is outside the east end of **Frome** parish church.

'Awake my soul' . . . these are appropriate words indeed for the new century, a century which was to prove a time of great evangelistic revival, and this advance can be attributed largely to an itinerant preacher riding on horseback with a devotional book, more than likely the Holy Bible, propped up in front of him. This seemingly indefatigable preacher was none other than John Wesley, who was born in 1703 and whose life was to span the century. His father was rector of **Epworth** in the fen country of what is now Humberside. John, who in his mother Susanna's eyes was called by God and 'a brand plucked from the burning', was one of ten children. At the age of five he was indeed rescued from a disastrous fire at the rectory. In his much acclaimed appraisal of Christianity, *The Christians,* Bamber Gascoigne presents some interesting statistics concerning John Wesley. He travelled one hundred miles each week, five thousand miles a year, the equivalent of nine times round the world in his lifetime, and he preached some forty thousand sermons. It is obvious that the number of places associated with John are extremely numerous and therefore the intention here is to mention a few of special interest. At **Oxford,** John was a student at Christ Church. From here he often visited the Kirkham family at **Stanton** Rectory, near Evesham.

Today, Christ Church, Oxford, a cathedral since the 1540s, is unique on several counts. It is one of the smallest cathedrals but has the largest diocese in England; it is the only cathedral church which is also a college chapel, and no one ever calls it Oxford Cathedral. Christ Church is known the world over and it owes its origin to a Saxon lady whose name means 'bond of peace' — Frideswide — who founded a place of prayer here in the eighth century. Alfred the Great himself met some clerics on the river-bank by the ford, and in consequence of the ensuing debate Oxford University was founded — according to an attractive legend. John Wesley must have passed this way often. Perhaps he thought of the Saxon saint and of Cardinal Wolsey, who, two hundred years before him, had had part of the nave pulled down in order to build 'Tom Quad' and Cardinal's College, as he called it. John was made a Fellow of Lincoln College and after an interval of a few years, when his brother Charles was at Oxford too, he returned.

It was about this time that Wesley's 'Bible moths group' and its 'holy club' members were ridiculed as Methodists. On 24th May 1738, whilst at a Christian house-meeting in **Aldersgate,** London, he felt his heart 'strangely warmed' by the love of God. This, he testifies, was the real moment of his conversion, a day recalled by Methodists everywhere. 'The brand plucked from the burning' thirty years before was on fire now. For the next fifty years he was to bring the gospel message to millions of people of all sorts and conditions, miners, weavers and smugglers, rich and poor, the deprived and the depraved. The world was his parish. At Hanham Mount, Kingswood, **Bristol,** memorial plaques recall his open-air preaching and also that of George Whitfield. In this same city is the celebrated New Room, the first Methodist chapel in the world. Cornwall warmed especially to John Wesley's preaching. Digory Isbell's cottage at **Trewint** near Altarnun and **Gwennap Pit,** where Methodists still gather on the terraced, grassy slopes, are two especially notable holy places on the Wesley trail. In the City Road, **London,** Wesley's Chapel, recently restored, dates from 1778. The holy mount of **Mow Cop** in Cheshire, sacred to Primitive Methodists, was the birthplace of a Nonconformist revival in 1807, sixteen years after Wesley's death. At the age of eighty-seven, not long before his death, John preached his last open-air sermon at **Winchelsea.** An ash tree in the churchyard of this charming Sussex town still marks the historic site.

George Whitfield, mentioned above, was born in **Gloucester** and converted at about the same time as John Wesley. He journeyed to America seven times in all. He also worked with Howell Harris, founder of Welsh Methodism, and co-operated with him in missionary tours in Wales. He also opened a preachers' college at **Trefeca** near Talgarth in Powys. This is still a religious centre and there is a museum. Whitfield founded the English Calvinistic Methodist Connexion, of which the famous Moorfields Chapel and the Tabernacle, Tottenham Court Road, were two notable **London** chapels. They were also known as the Countess of Huntingdon's Connexion. The Countess Selina, the 'Teresa of the

Methodists', was a patroness of the revival and her college at Trefeca and her private chapels enabled the gospel to be preached to the well-to-do. In 1740, in Scotland, George Whitfield preached to forty thousand and this marks the Revival of **Cambuslang** near Glasgow. As a result of this, Dr John Erskine, who was greatly influenced, ministered faithfully for sixty years at Greyfriars Church in **Edinburgh.**

A notable Anglican evangelical was Augustus Toplady, whose hymn 'Rock of Ages' was inspired by a cleft in a rock where he sheltered from a storm over **Burrington Combe** in the Mendip Hills. That was in the 1770s. At the close of this decade the one-time slave trader John Newton and the meditative William Cowper produced many hymns which have come to be treasured; the collection, which includes 'How sweet the name of Jesus sounds' and 'Jesus, where'er thy people meet', is named after the small town of **Olney** in north Buckinghamshire, famous for its Shrove Tuesday pancake race. Here the river Ouse, reflecting the tall spired church, meanders across the low undulating countryside. The *Olney Hymns* and other mementoes are displayed at the Cowper Memorial Museum in the market place. Hymnody has long been a vehicle for great Christian truths; the hymns of the Wesleys run into hundreds, some say thousands, and assert the saying that Methodism was 'born in song' — 'O for a thousand tongues to sing', proclaims Charles. It is, however, Isaac Watts of **Southampton** who is generally regarded as the Father of English Hymns. As a lad he was scolded and begged for pardon in verse! 'Father, father, pity take and I will no more verses make.' Fortunately for us he was encouraged to write and so today we can sing 'When I survey the wondrous cross', probably the best known passiontide hymn. 'O God our help in ages past' sounds forth from the civic centre chimes in his home town. Number 41 French Street was his birthplace and a new United Reformed church, the Isaac Watts Memorial Church, perpetuates the name of this popular hymn writer and preacher; the Congregational branch of the church can proudly lay claim to him as one of its most celebrated sons.

In 1782 the spotlight was turned on the university city of **Cambridge,** where a young clergyman became vicar of Holy Trinity. He was Charles Simeon, whose evangelical fervour was to revolutionise mission at home and abroad. It is helpful to remember that the religious origins of colleges such as those at Cambridge and Oxford are conveyed in their layout in that the college chapels remind one of medieval monastic establishments with choir stalls facing each other. It was the great cathedral schools which led to the founding of universities and the latter could therefore be regarded as holy places where, according to

Peter Abelard, the medieval French scholar and teacher, 'the first key to wisdom is this constant and frequent questioning . . . (to) arrive at the truth'.

The late 1770s saw the inauguration of an idea which led to the founding of the first Sunday school or rather school on Sunday, since children worked in factories during the week. Robert Raikes of **Gloucester** and a few others sowed the seed for providing day schools all over Britain. A memorial in Brunswick Street commemorates Robert Raikes's 'Sunday school' in St Catherine Street. In 1777 the Reverend Thomas Stock gathered children for free education in the chancel of **Ashbury** church in Oxfordshire. Later this 'Sunday school' had its own premises close by. Here today are visible reminders of the origins of free education in Britain. Thomas Stock worked closely with Robert Raikes.

9. 1800 to the present day

Onward, Christian soldiers

The day before he died John Wesley wrote a letter to William Wilberforce encouraging him in his fight against slavery. Five years before William sat with his friend William Pitt beneath a tree at Holwood overlooking the Keston valley in Kent and told him he had decided to lead the fight against slavery and the slave trade. The law was finally passed in 1833. The reformer's birthplace at 25 High Street in **Kingston-upon-Hull** is now a museum portraying his life's work. William was a member of the Clapham Sect, a body of Christian reformers who met at the home of Granville Sharp in **Clapham,** London. William Wilberforce was also the vice-president of the Church Missionary Society founded in 1799.

The Tolpuddle Martyrs were a group of six Dorset labourers led by a Methodist, George Loveless, all sentenced to transportation for forming a union in 1834. The village of **Tolpuddle** is a place of pilgrimage, with its TUC cottages and the famous Martyrs' Tree, an ailing sycamore, down the road from the chapel with its memorial plaque.

Just before the turn of the century at **Kettering** in Northamptonshire a Baptist aged thirty-one, William Carey, founded the Baptist Missionary Society. The Mission House associated with this historic event is in Lower Street. The nineteenth century was a time of great missionary expansion overseas. There were many notable men and women involved in this work but possibly none is so famous as David Livingstone, whose birthplace (in 1813), a tenement at **Blantyre** near Glasgow, is now his national memorial with a comprehensive display of personal relics.

Robert Owen, by birth a Welshman of Newtown, believed in a philanthropic approach in business and his New Lanark Mill became famous for its welfare schemes.

In 1804 the British and Foreign Bible Society was started. This grew out of one man's concern for the provision of bibles in Welsh. His name was Thomas Charles, a minister of **Bala** in North Wales, where his memorial can be seen near Tegid Chapel. The seed of his concern was sown by a little girl, Mary Jones, who walked through the mountains a distance of twenty-five miles from **Llanfihangel** to Bala in order to buy a bible. Llanfihangel y Pennant commemorates Mary by a monument near the bridge. Here too are the ruins of the house in which she was born.

Whilst in North Wales the pilgrim should visit a holy place associated with another young girl. For many hundreds of years the famous healing well of St Winifride at **Holywell** has drawn the devout to this Lourdes of Britain, which, with its chapel, churches and hospice, is an outstanding Christian centre.

One of the strengths, and perhaps weaknesses too, of the Church of England has been its all embracing nature; this is probably a good thing for an established church since it enables a wide range of gifts to thrive and also colour in churchmanship to grow side by side. The Church of England has also assumed, for some people at least, the function of a bridge church linking the extremes of the various denominations. A holy, catholic (meaning universal) and apostolic church was the aim of a movement known as the Tractarian Revival. It was also called the **Oxford** Movement since it began in Oriel College, Oxford, and it emphasised tradition and sacrament. It was as much a revival as the Evangelical Revival before it. A scholarly man, John Keble, born at **Fairford** in Gloucestershire in 1792, became vicar of **Hursley** near Winchester. It was his sermon on national apostasy in the 1830s that instigated the movement. He had been professor of poetry at Oxford. His most notable work was a volume of devotional verse, *The Christian Year*. Hymns of his, like 'Blest are the pure in heart', are still popular. A college at Oxford is named after him. Other celebrated workers in the Movement were E. S. Pusey and John Henry Newman, well known for his hymn 'Lead, kindly light'. Light and life were certainly what the Church of England needed at this time since it was in a sad state. At Hursley, where John Keble is buried, he beautified the church and made his parish a place of Christian compassion. Three years after his death in 1866 a fifty-year-old Devon-born man became a chaplain to Queen Victoria. He was Charles Kingsley, a much respected country parson at **Eversley,** also in Hampshire. He made his mark in the world of reform, preaching and writing, but most of all he was a Christian Socialist. He loved the young and was concerned about a better society, a true 'fisher of men'. His grave is in the churchyard of the eighteenth-century brick church at Eversley, his only living for thirty years; nearby is his vicarage.

London's most famous statue, the Angel of Christian Charity (not Eros) is in Piccadilly. At the hub of the British Empire (as it used to be said) this commemorates Lord Shaftesbury, the philanthropist, founder of ragged schools and campaigner for the poor. Shaftesbury Avenue also commemorates him.

Nottinghamshire-born William Booth began his own mission in a tent at **Whitechapel** in London in 1865. This was the beginning of the Salvation Army and in those early days the 'Army' met much opposition. Nowadays it is respected everywhere.

In the year of Lord Shaftesbury's death an Act of Parliament authorised the building of what has come to be called one of the noblest churches in Christendom. **Liverpool** Cathedral in all its vastness rises above industrial Merseyside. Its completion in 1978 was marked by a great service of dedication and praise in the presence of Her Majesty the Queen.

The Diocese of **Truro** was formed in the late 1870s and the first part of the beautiful new cathedral in Truro was consecrated in 1887. Bishop Edward White Benson, later Archbishop, was a much loved pastor. He devised the now world-famous service of Nine Lessons and Carols, first used in his humble makeshift 'cathedral' in 1880. He went to **Gwennap Pit** soon after his enthronement and, standing where John Wesley had stood, prayed for Christian unity.

Dance, then, wherever you may be

Christian unity and reconciliation are much to the fore at **Coventry**, where the new mid twentieth-century cathedral seeks to make a break with tradition and yet still to remain rooted in great Christian truths. There is much symbolism in the modern furnishings and architectural features: old and new side by side, death and resurrection, forgiveness and reconciliation.

Liverpool and **Guildford** are the only two Anglican cathedrals built on new sites in Britain since the middle ages. High on Stag Hill, Guildford Cathedral is dedicated to the Holy Spirit. A short distance away the ancient **Pilgrims' Way** from Winchester to Canterbury passes to the top of another hill where St Martha's Church recalls martyrdom and sacrifice.

Two outstanding cathedral churches of our own times which break with the Gothic tradition and enable the gathering of the Lord's people around the Lord's Table in a particularly telling way are Roman Catholic ones. The cathedral in **Liverpool** has an interior bathed in light from the Ely-like lantern, the focal point being the central altar. At **Clifton** in Bristol the Roman Catholic cathedral is of another imaginative design based on a hexagon and equilateral triangles — simple, severe, nothing pretentious; it was said on its consecration in 1973 to have been the ecclesiastical bargain of the century.

A visit to the great Christian centre at **Buckfast** Abbey in Devon should be enriched by the knowledge that it was all built in the twentieth century by amateurs for the most part, with a trained stone-mason, a staggering achievement and an inspiring act of faith. The site was first settled in the eleventh century. The monastic tradition continues here as indeed it does in many other holy places up and down Britain, places which the pilgrim tourist will wish to respect for their very special nature. At Buckfast, however, visitors are catered for. There is much to enrich one's experience, backed by the memorable tolling of the bell at certain times.

Aylesford Friary in Kent is much visited by Christians of various denominations. Here, one Christmas in the 1240s, St Simon Stock and a band of White Friars started the first Carmelite house in England. In 1949 the house was re-established and the body of St Simon was brought from Bordeaux. Hospitality and the welcoming of pilgrims continue today.

Derwent Water, **Keswick,** is the venue for the famous Christian convention every summer. From small beginnings in 1875 this annual assembly for the deepening of the spiritual life has brought inestimable blessing to thousands. For such the specially erected tents where 'all are one in Christ Jesus' are indeed holy places.

Brother Douglas, a modern St Francis, was the prior of the Brotherhood of St Francis, which sought to help the wayfaring folk — the beggars and unemployed of the 1930s. Flowers Farm at Hilfield, remote in the country near **Cerne Abbas** in Dorset, is one of several houses of the Society of St Francis. Another notable modern monastery where they 'pray devoutly and hammer stoutly' is **Mount St Bernard** in Charnwood Forest, Leicestershire, founded in 1848, with Dom Bernard Palmer its first abbot.

When considering these many and varied expressions of the Christian faith one may well ask: what of Christian unity? The modern ecumenical movement dates from a missionary conference held in **Edinburgh** in 1910 and culminating in the World Council of Churches, founded in Amsterdam in 1948. There are occasions too when Christian and non-Christian alike, the half believers and the doubters on life's pilgrimage, are somehow united, emotionally at least, when some awe-inspiring event takes place in a national shrine like **St Paul's Cathedral** or Westminster Abbey. Wren's masterpiece replaced one of our largest medieval cathedrals, destroyed in the Great Fire of London. It was far back in 604, however, that Mellitus was made bishop by St Augustine and King Ethelbert of Kent founded the first St Paul's for him. The present massive domed building is the fifth cathedral here.

10. Full circle

From east to west, from shore to shore

We shall end this pilgrimage where we began — on a hill in Hertfordshire. It seems quite natural to have come full circle, back to a most potent and significant holy place, the shrine of Britain's first Christian martyr.

The abbey church at **St Albans** is a good example of a pilgrimage church which is now not only a cathedral but also a parish church with a large regular congregation from which there is a steady flow of personnel with varied gifts who voluntarily help to man a wide range of activities and organisations. Back in the thirteenth and fourteenth centuries the Benedictine monastery here had a high reputation for its school of painters. The murals or wall paintings here in Europe's longest medieval nave are still amongst the finest in the world. St Albans, moreover, was at one time the premier abbey of England. One of many great names is Matthew Paris, the chronicler, who was a monk here between 1217 and 1259; he took the best advantage of the abbey's proximity to London, only a day's journey away. Kings, nobles, bishops and other important people were frequently guests and so Matthew wrote his entertaining chronicle, an illuminating record of events. The shrine of St Alban was a focal point for medieval travellers on the pilgrim routes. The tradition continues as people of many creeds, races and Christian denominations, drawn by the great red brick Norman tower, gather for fellowship, dialogue and Christian studies at the place where Britain's first martyr died. Events such as Festivals of Youth and the International Organ Festival are becoming more and more part of the Church's ecumenical outreach. A new age in the life of the Abbey has begun with the building of the new Chapter House and Visitors' Centre on the old medieval site.

In the twelfth century St Albans gave the world the only English Pope, Nicholas Breakspear, Adrian IV. At the start of the 1980s Robert Runcie, the seventh bishop of St Albans (the abbey has only been a cathedral church since the late nineteenth century) was chosen as the one hundred and second Archbishop of Canterbury. The pilgrimage continues.

> Thy kingdom come! On bended knee
>   The passing ages pray.
> And faithful souls have yearned to see
>   On earth that kingdom's day.

Gazetteer and maps

The main object of interest at the places which are listed here and which are not described in the text is, unless otherwise stated, the church or chapel. These places are shown on the maps by means of infilled black circles. Places which are mentioned in the text are shown on the maps by means of crosses and readers should consult the index to find the reference. The reader will appreciate that most of the places mentioned, in whatever category, are of interest for more than one reason. There are also countless other churches, chapels, shrines and holy places to be discovered. The pilgrim tourist will always wish to respect the very special nature and privacy of religious communities.

Abbreviations: c – chapel or meeting house; cath – cathedral; ch – church; co – community; m – medieval; N – Norman; r – ruin; S – Saxon.

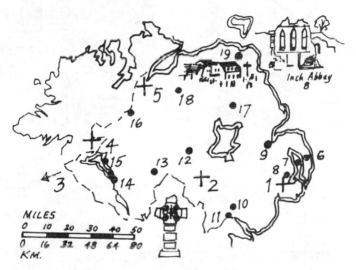

Northern Ireland

Places mentioned in the text, numbered 1-5 on the map
Armagh 2. Croagh Patrick 3. Downpatrick 1. Londonderry 5. Lough Derg 4.

Some other places with interesting associations
Corrymeela, near Ballycastle, co dedicated to reconciliation 19. Gracehill, near Ballymena, Moravian settlement 17.

Some other places of mainly architectural interest
Belfast, two caths 9. Clogher cath 13. Donaghmore Cross 12. Dungiven Priory 18. Enniskillen, cath and Devenish Island r and round tower 14. Grey Abbey r 6. Inch Abbey r 8. Killeavy, two r ch 11. Nendrum r 7. Newry, RC cath and oldest Protestant ch 10. Strabane, modern RC ch 16. White Island and Killadeas (graveyard) 15.

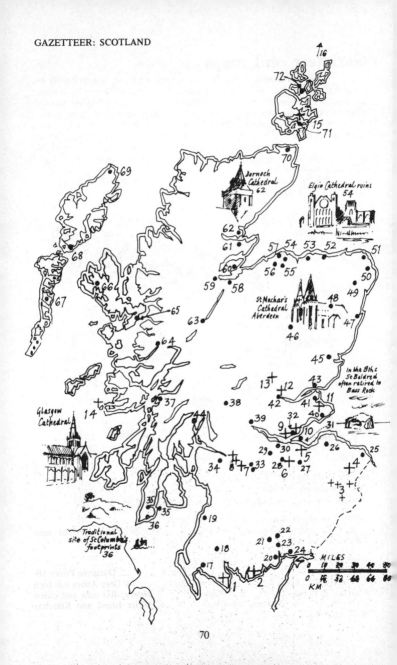

Scotland
Places mentioned in the text, numbered 1-16 on the map
Blantyre 7. Border abbeys (Dryburgh, Jedburgh, Kelso, Melrose) 3. Burntisland 10.
Cambuslang 8. Dundrennan 2. Dunfermline 9. Dunkeld 13. Duns 4. Edinburgh 5.
Glasgow 8. Iona 14. Kirkwall 15. Mid Calder House 6. St Andrews 11. Scone 12.
Shetland 16. Whithorn 1.

Some other places with interesting associations
Balquhidder (Rob Roy) 38. Buchie and Chapelford (RC stronghold) 53. Burghead
(Roman well and New Year ceremony) 57. Cairnbulg (festival 5th Jan) 51. Crathie
(Royal Family) 46. Crimond (hymn tune Ps 23) 50. Dumfries (Bruce) 23. Fort
Augustus Abbey co 63. Glen Trool (Covenanters Memorial) 18. Glenfinnan
Monument (Prince Charlie) 64. Keil (St Columba) 36. Kilmuir (Flora MacDonald)
66. Lamb Holm (Italian chapel) 71. Livingston (ecumenical, shared church) 28.
Lochgoilhead (Three Holy Brethren) 44. Old Monkland 33. Perth (cath; John Knox
Reformation sermon) 42. Pluscarden Priory co 56. Southend (Keil; St Columba) 36.
Stirling (Virgin Martyrs' memorial) 39. Tain (St Duthac) 61. Whitehills (St Brandon)
r 52.

Some other places of mainly architectural interest
Aberdeen cath 47. Aberdour 32. Beauly Priory r 59. Birnie (N gem) 55. Brechin cath
45. Butt of Lewis, St Moluag 69. Campbelltown, St Kiaren's Cave; Davaar Island,
Crucifixion painting in cave 35. Canisbay 70. Carfin, RC grotto 33. Coldingham
Priory 25. Crossraguel r 19. Deer Abbey r 49. Dornoch cath 62. Dunblane cath 39.
Dundee (three chs, one roof) 43. Egilsay r 72. Elgin cath r 54. Fortrose cath and r
60. Glenluce r 17. Haddington (Lamp of the Lothians; John Knox) 26. Inchcolm
Island (Iona of the east, r) 31. Inverness cath 58. Kirk Patrick Irongray (obelisk;
sculptures) 21. Leuchars (N gem) 41. Lincluden Abbey r; a gem 22. Linlithgow
(m gem) 30. Monymusk 48. Oban, two caths 37. Oronsay Island r 65. Paisley
Abbey and Baptist ch, 'finest in Europe' 34. Pittenweem r 40. Rodel, old church 68.
Rosslyn (Roslin) Chapel 27. Ruthwell Cross 24. St Monance 40. South Uist, Our
Lady of the Isles 67. Sweetheart Abbey r; a gem 20. Torphichen, Knights
Hospitallers 29.

71

MILES
0 10 20 30 40 50
0 16 32 48 64 80
KM.

Marking the way for
Pilgrims to the
Holy Island of Lindisfarne

+25
•60

•57

Hexham
Abbey
+24
•59 +
58 •23
+22

Tomb of
Saint Cuthbert
Durham Cathedral
21

+21
•50

+20
Swarthmoor Hall
•51

•49

+15

•55
•54
•53
•52
+18

Ancient crypt
at Ripon

•48

•47

+17
+16

+13
+14

•19
•46

•12 +11

+44 Central
Tower
York
•10

•45

+43

+9

Pendle Hill
•7

•38

•39

•40

•41

+8

+5

•35

+42

ISLE
OF
MAN
•63
62•   •64
•61

+6

Two contrasting
towers in
Liverpool

•37
•36

•34 +4

+3 +2

Lincoln's great
towers

•27
•26

•33

•31
•30
•32   •29
•28

+1

Northern England

Places mentioned in the text, numbered 1-25 on the map

Beverley 9. Brigg Flatts 18. Durham 21. Epworth 4. Fountains 12. Gainsborough 2. Hexham 24. Jarrow 23. Keswick 20. Kingston upon Hull 8. Lastingham 14. Lincoln 1. Lindisfarne (Holy Island) 25. Liverpool 6. Monkwearmouth 22. Mount Grace 17. Osmotherley 16. Pendle Hill 7. Rievaulx 13. Ripon 11. Scrooby 3. Swarthmoor 19. Wakefield 5. Whitby 15. York 10.

Some other places with interesting associations

Ampleforth (school co) 44. Bamburgh (Oswald, Aidan) 60. Castletown (crucifix) 61. Eyam (plague village) 31. Firbank (Fox's pulpit) 52. Grindleford (Martyrs' c) 30. Knaresborough (shrine) 45.

Some other places of mainly architectural interest

Barton on Humber S 35. Bewcastle Cross 57. Blackburn cath 38. Bradford cath 39. Bridlington Priory 43. Carlisle cath 56. Cartmel Priory 53. Chesterfield 29. Darlington 49. Doncaster 34. Escomb (S gem) 50. Gawsworth 36. Gosforth Cross 55. Gibside c 58. Jervaulx r 47. Keld c 51. Kirk Maughold 64. Kirk Michael 63. Lancaster 46. Leeds RC cath; Kirkstall Abbey 40. Louth (spire) 27. Manchester cath 37. Newcastle cath 59. Patrington (m gem) 42. Peel 62. Richmond 48. Selby (N gem) 41. Shap Abbey r 51. Sheffield cath 33. Theddlethorpe All Saints 26. Tideswell (Cathedral of the Peak) 32. Ulpha (see Wordsworth's poem) 54. Worksop Priory 28.

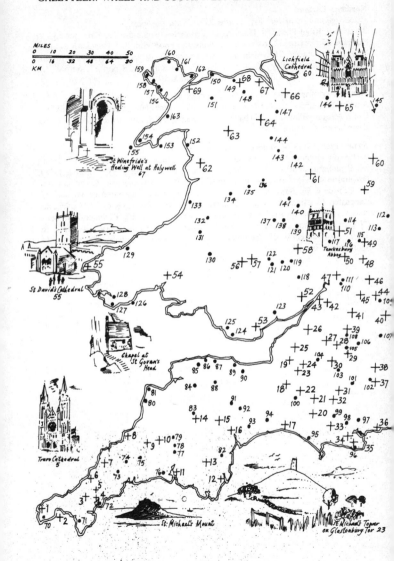

Wales and South-west England

Places mentioned in the text, numbered 1-69 on the map

Amesbury 38. Ashbury 40. Athelney 18. Bala 63. Bangor 69. Bath 27. Bemerton 37. Berkeley 43. Birmingham (and 2 caths) 59. Burrington Combe 25. Bradford on Avon 28. Brecon 56. Bristol 26. Buckfast 13. Carmarthen 54. Cerne Abbas 20. Chester 66. Chippenham 39. Christchurch 36. Cirencester 45. Clifton 26. Come-to-Good 4. Corfe 35. Crediton 15. Dartmouth 12. Edington 29. Exeter 16. Fairford 44. Frome 30. Glastonbury 23. Gloucester 47. Gwennap Pit 3. Hayles 48. Hereford 58. Hinton St Mary 32. Holywell 67. Ilchester 22. Lanherne 7. Launceston 10. Lichfield 60. Llandaff 53. Llanfihangel 62. Longleat 30. Malmesbury 41. Mow Cop 65. Much Wenlock 61. Nibley Knoll 42. Northleach 46. Plymouth (and St Andrew's) 11. St Asaph 68. St David's 55. St Just 1. St Michael's Mount 2. St Pyran in the Sand 6. Salisbury 37. Sampford Courtenay 14. Shaftesbury 31. Sherborne 21. Stanton 49. Tewkesbury 50. Tintagel 8. Tintern 52. Tolpuddle 33. Trefeca 57. Trewint 9. Truro 5. Valle Crucis 64. Wareham 34. Wedmore 19. Wells 24. Whitchurch Canoricorum 17. Winchcombe 48. Worcester 51.

Some other places with interesting associations

Aberdaron (pilgrims) 154. Bardsey Island (20,000 saints) 155. Bodmin (Guron, Petroc) 74. Caldy Island co 126. Chittlehampton (St Urith) 84. Clynnog Fawr (St Beuno) 163. Droitwich (St Richard) 114. Great Orme (St Tudno) 150. Lee Abbey co 86. Lew Trenchard (hymns) 79. Llanddewi Brefi (St David) 131. Llandovery (hymns) 130. Llangorwen (Keble) 133. Llanidloes (Wesley) 134. Montacute 100. Montgomery (Herbert) 136. Morwenstow (Hawker) 80. Nanteos (Holy Grail) 133. Newtown (Owen) 135. Oswestry (Oswald) 144. Prinknash co 111. St Levan 70. St Tudwal Island 153. Wardour RC 101. Wilton 102.

Some other places of mainly architectural interest

Abbey Dore 120. Abbotsbury r and c 95. Aberffraw 156. Amlwch RC 160. Bodelwyddan 149. Bosherston 127. Brent Tor 78. Capel y Ffin 122. Chapel Plaister (Box) c 108. Cheadle RC 145. Cleeve Abbey r 90. Culbone 87. Cullompton 92. Denbigh 148. Devizes 106. Downside RC 104. Dunster 89. Evesham 115. Ewenny 125. Great Malvern 117. Gunwalloe 71. Hartland 81. Holy Island 159. Honeychurch 83. Horningsham c 103. Inglesham 109. Kilpeck 119. Lacock 108. Leamington Spa 112. Leominster 139. Loughwood c 94. Llanallgo r 161. Llandanwg 152. Llanfair yn Neubwll 158. Llangwyfan 157. Llanrwst 151. Llanthony Priory r 121. Llantwit Major 124. Ludlow 140. Marlborough 107. Melverley 143. Milton Abbas 99. Mullion 88. Monmouth r 118. Nevern 129. Newport cath 123. Newton Abbot, dream ch 82. Ottery St Mary 93. Painswick 110. Parracombe 85. Pembroke 128. Penmon 162. Pershore 116. Presteigne, priest's hole 137. Roche Rock r and c 73. St Aldhelm's Head c 96. St Germans 76. St Govan's Head c 127. St Just in Roseland 72. St Neot 75. Sandbach 146. Shobdon 138. Shrewsbury 142. Steeple Ashton 105. Stokesay 141. Strata Florida Abbey r 132. Stratford upon Avon 113. Tavistock 77. Tissington (well dressing) 145. Tiverton 91. Warwick 112. Wimborne Minster 97. Winterborne Tomson 98. Wrexham 147.

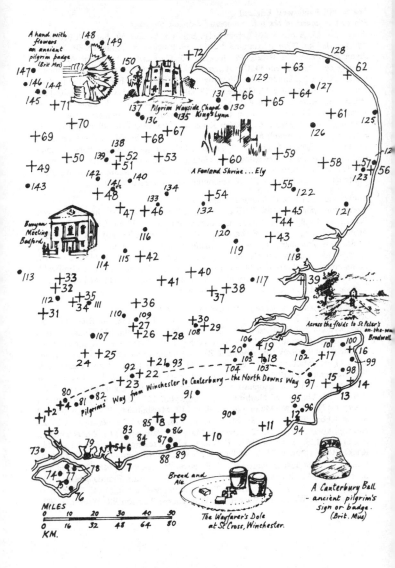

A hand with flowers an ancient pilgrim badge (Brit Mus)

Pilgrim Wayside Chapel ... King's Lynn

A Fenland Shrine ... Ely

Bunyan Meeting Bedford.

Across the fields to St Peter's on-the-wall Bradwell.

Pilgrims' Way from Winchester to Canterbury — the North Downs Way

A Canterbury Bell — ancient pilgrim's sign or badge. (Brit. Mus)

Bread and Ale

MILES
0   10   20   30   40   50
0   16   32   48   64   80
KM.

The Wayfarer's Dole at St Cross, Winchester.

76

South-east England

Places mentioned in the text, numbered 1-72 on the map

Aylesford 18. Battle 11. Bedford 46. Bosham 5. Boston 72. Bradwell 39. Bromholm 62. Bury St Edmunds 55. Cambridge (and college chapels) 54. Canterbury 17. Castle Acre 65. Chalfont St Giles 36. Chalgrove 35. Chichester 6. Coolham 8. Coventry 49. Cowfold 9. Dorchester on Thames 34. Dover 14. Dunstable 42. Dunwich 56. Ebbsfleet 16. Ely 60. Eton 27. Eversley 25. Fenny Drayton 69. Folkestone 13. Fotheringhay 68. Geddington 52. Greenwich 29. Greensted juxta Ongar 38. Guildford 22. Hampton Court 28. Hertford 40. Hoxne 58. Hursley 2. Jordans 36. Kettering 51. King's Lynn 66. Lavenham 45. Leicester (and cath) 70. Lewes 10. Little Gidding 53. Little Maplestead 43. London 30. Long Melford 44. Lullingstone 20. Lutterworth 50. Lyminge 15. Mount St Bernard 71. North Elmham 64. Northampton 48. Norwich 61. Ockham 21. Olney 47. Oxford (and college chapels) 33. Peterborough 67. Rochester 19. Romsey 1. Runnymede 26. St Albans 41. St Cross 4. St Martha's 22. Selsey 7. Silchester 24. Southampton 3. Sunningwell 32. Thetford 59. Walpole 57. Walsingham 63. Waltham Abbey 37. Wantage 31. Waverley 23. Winchelsea 12. Winchester 4. Windsor 27.

Some other places with interesting associations

Ampthill (Bunyan's House Beautiful) 116. Carisbrooke (Castle – Charles I) 74. Cookham (Stanley Spencer paintings) 110. Crowland (St Guthlac) 135. Faversham (King Stephen) 102. Hartley (RC co) 106. Kemsing (Abbess Edith) 104. Lancing school c 87. Mayfield (Dunstan) 90. Minster in Thanet (Abbess Mildred) co 100. North Marston (John Shorne, priest) 114. Quarr Abbey co 78. Sandringham (Royal Family) 129. Selborne (Gilbert White, naturalist) 82. Steyning (St Cuthman) 86. Stoke Poges (Gray's Elegy) 109. Storrington RC co (Francis Thompson) 85. Tichborne (dole) 81.

Some other places of mainly architectural interest.

Abingdon 112. Arundel RC cath 84. Barfreston (N gem) 98. Beaulieu r and museum 73. Blythburgh 123. Bonchurch 76. Boxgrove Priory 83. Breedon on the Hill 144. Brixworth (S gem) 142. Brookland 96. Burford 113. Chelmsford cath 117. Colchester r 118. Compton (Pilgrims' Way) 92. Cromer 128. Derby cath 147. Dode c 105. Earls Barton S 141. East Guldeford 94. Ewelme 111. Fairfield (marshland gem) 95. Godshill 75. Grantham (m gem) 150. Great Yarmouth 125. Haslingfield (Chapel Hill) 132. Headbourne Worthy 80. Higham Ferrers 140. Kenilworth 143. Leighton Buzzard 115. London: Southwark cath, Westminster RC cath, All Hallows by the Tower (Toc H), Wren churches, All Souls by BBC (evangelical witness) 108. Maidstone 103. Newark 149. Portsmouth cath 79. Reading r 107. Reculver r 101. Repton S 146. Rothwell 139. Roxton c 133. Rushton 138. Rye 94. Saffron Walden 120. St Neots 134. Salle (m gem) 127. Sandwich 99. Shere 93. Shoreham (2 gems) 89. Sompting S 88. Southwell cath 148. Southwold 124. Stamford 136. Staunton Harold 145. Thaxted 119. Tickencote (N gem) 137. Ufford (font cover) 121. Walpole St Peter 131. Whippingham 77. Wiggenhalls (three) 130. Woolpit (roof) 122. Worth S and RC school c 91. Wye 97. Wymondham 126.

Index

INDEX